THINK LIKE A BOSS!

Most people go to a job interview thinking they are the underdog; that the prospective boss is cool, calm, collected and in control. Nothing could be further from the truth. Bosses are nervous! Bosses hate hiring almost as much as you hate job hunting! They will do anything to avoid the grueling, risky, and time-consuming hiring process. They're desperately hoping you will be the one who can help them out of the bind they're in. But what do most job seekers do? They go into an interview as if they are saying, "HELP ME! EMPLOY ME! I NEED A JOB!"

What they should be saying is, "What do you need? How can I help you?" If you can think like a boss and make a prospective employer feel that you care about this job, that you will make his or her life easier, and if you can convince the employer that you have what he or she is really looking for, then you'll get a job offer every time.

Other books in the *Smart Questions* series

Smart Questions to Ask Your Doctor
Smart Questions to Ask Your Lawyer
Smart Questions to Ask Your Insurance Agent
Smart Questions to Ask Your Stockbroker
*Smart Questions to Ask About Your Children's Education

*coming soon

Published by
HarperPaperbacks

SMART QUESTIONS:

INTERVIEW YOUR WAY TO JOB SUCCESS

DOROTHY LEEDS

HarperPaperbacks
A Division of HarperCollinsPublishers

HarperPaperbacks   *A Division of* HarperCollins*Publishers*
10 East 53rd Street, New York, N.Y. 10022

Cover design by Richard Rossiter

First printing: October 1993

Printed in the United States of America

HarperPaperbacks and colophon are trademarks of
HarperCollins*Publishers*

❖ 10 9 8 7 6 5 4 3 2 1

To my talented, beautiful, loving, and caring sister, Gloria Strauss. She started it all by giving me my very first grown-up books. Thank you, Gloria, for everything, always.

ACKNOWLEDGMENTS

Special thanks to Marvin Berenblum, Gloria Kessler, Patricia O'Leary, Rachel Philipp, and Jill Rosenfeld.

And a special note of appreciation to Sharyn Kolberg, whose diligence, patience, fortitude, calm demeanor, and excellent writing skills make it all seem easy.

CONTENTS

A MUST-READ INTRODUCTION

WHY YOU NEED THIS BOOK

Because good jobs are hard to find. Because when you do find a good job, someone else always seems to get it. Because you always end up with a job that depresses you, a boss you hate, and/or a feeling of being stuck in a rut with the ways out getting fewer and farther between.

If these are your perceptions of what your working life is like, you need to do something about it. READ THIS BOOK. This is the *only* book that will teach the two things you need to know most: *how to ask the questions* that will get you the information you need, and *how to use every available type of interview—from networking to negotiation—to locate, explore, and land you the jobs you really want.*

The purpose of this book is threefold:

1. To provide you with the questions to ask in order get "the real story" about the job, the company, and the prospective boss;

2. To get you into the habit of asking questions; and
3. To educate you about and encourage you to use all the interview opportunities available to you.

Perhaps most important, however, this book is designed to give you the confidence you need not just to survive, but to flourish in tough economic times.

There have been tough times and periods of high unemployment before. But never before has unemployment been so unilateral—executives and professionals are now just as likely to be out of work as assistants or unskilled or manufacturing staff.

No matter what your level of previous employment, you need to hone your interviewing skills. In fact, the higher lever you are, the more people will expect of you at an interview. If you're looking for a mangerial position, you may not go through an employment agency or personnel-department interview. However, it's almost impossible in these times to obtain a high-level position without strong networking abilities. And it's likely that you'll be interviewed by headhunters.

Everyone who is looking for a job faces an interview situation somewhere along the line. The more you know about the interviewing process, the greater the chances *you* will be a candidate employers are hoping to find.

The basic priciples of interviewing apply no matter what your level. If you're just beginning, this book will serve as a primer and guide. If you've recently been laid off or fired, this book will serve as a refresher course.

THE SINGLE INTERVIEW MYTH

There are a few things about interviews that I'd like to clear up right away. First, it's important to recognize that there are *many different types* of interviews. We usually think of "the interview"—the one where you're talking directly to the person who may be hiring you. However, there are other kinds of interviews we often ignore. These include:

- *The Information Interview:* In this interview, you're looking for information rather than asking for a job. This is one of the strongest marketing tools available to job seekers—and one of the least utilized. Information interviews are especially useful if you're new to the job market, or are changing from one field to another, and don't know many details about the industry that is new to you. The object at information interviews is not necessarily to get a job offer, but to fill in the gaps in your knowledge.
- *The Networking or Referral Interview:* Statistics show that up to 80 percent of all new jobs are found through networking. Networking interviews can be formal or informal. A formal networking interview may take place in an office setting; an informal interview may take place anywhere at all. When you are looking for a job, you should be networking all the time. This book reveals the secrets of both subtle and overt networking, and helps you start a networking notebook so that you can uncover your own trail of job-search connections.
- *The Employment-Agency Interview:* The most important thing to remember about employment agencies is that they make money by getting people jobs. Any jobs. They are not necessarily interested in getting you the kind of job you want. This book will show you how to take control of the agency interview, be very specific about your needs, and get the kinds of job interviews you want.
- *The Headhunter Interview:* This is the only category where the interviewer generally calls you first. But

even headhunters have to get your name from some-where, and you want to be sure you're on their list. How do you do this? By marketing and promoting yourself. You'll learn some of the ways to make your-self visible so that headhunters are likely to think of you first when job openings arise. You'll also discover when you should call (or write) the headhunter first; what to do when the headhunter calls you; when to continue the conversation and when to set up a meet-ing; typical questions a headhunter will ask; and what questions you should ask the headhunter.

•*The Personnel-Department Interview*: This is the one type of interview you want to try to avoid. However, this is not always possible—especially for entry-level jobs in large companies. Personnel's job is twofold: to weed people out and to find the person who most perfectly matches the boss's require-ments. The personnel interviewer doesn't want to send an obviously unqualified candidate to the man-ager who is looking for an employee. She's going to look at your résumé and your job qualifications in order to try to find the perfect fit, and any devia-tions are going to make a negative impression. As long as you understand the purpose of this kind of interview, you can learn how to get personnel on your side, how to sell your strengths, and how to tell the interviewer what she needs to hear in order to pass you on to the real decision maker.

•*The Preinterview Interview:* Whether you realize it or not, you may go through a screening interview by a secretary or receptionist when you call to set up an interview appointment. We'll let you in on specific techniques for dealing with this situation, and reveal other secrets such as the best times to call, how to use the telephone operator as your personal secretary, and how to use the preinterview to get information about the job.

- *The Callback Interview:* You've had one interview and it went very well—so well that the interviewer has asked you to come back a second time. What do you do now? You'll learn how to take advantage of this situation to find out more details about the company and the people with whom you may be working, how to shine a second time with the same interviewer, and how to deal with an interview with another person in the company (the interviewer's supervisor, partner, or associate).

- *The Multiple-Employer Interview:* It's difficult enough to walk into a room and face a total stranger for a job interview. What happens when you walk in and there are *three or four* strangers facing you all in a row? This situation can be pretty intimidating— unless you're prepared in advance. How you handle yourself under these circumstances is not that different from a normal interview. You'll learn how to establish a rapport with each of the interviewers, how to relax under stress, and how to ask and answer questions from the "group."

If you know how to handle yourself in these situations, you'll be a pro by the time you're interviewed by the person who counts the most.

LOOKING FOR WORK IN HARD TIMES

There was a time not so long ago when jobs were plentiful. Of course, not everyone got the job of their dreams, but you could pretty much count on getting a job somewhere within your field of interest. And, especially if you went to one of the "better" schools, you were almost guaranteed employment right after graduation.

Now, because of the complicated economic times in which we live, a college degree and/or an impressive résumé guarantee nothing. Thousands of people are being laid off every week, and the competition for available jobs is strong and fierce. Is this the death of the American dream?

I don't believe so. True, we're living in difficult times. But if you're willing to do a little bit more than the average job seeker, if you're willing to take that extra initiative, you can get the kind of job you really want. How do you know what that "little bit more" is? How do you know where to find the jobs you want? How do you know what will make an employer want to hire you above all the other qualified applicants for the job? You don't know . . . unless you ask questions!

There are three categories of questions contained in this book.

1. Questions about the interviewing process itself: what you need to know and how you can go about getting the information you need.
2. Questions you need to ask yourself: analyzing your own skills and experiences, as well as your needs and desires, so that you can present yourself to interviewers as well prepared and self-confident.
3. Questions you need to ask interviewers: You're not only trying to get a job offer, you're trying to get enough information about the job so that you can make an informed decision about whether or not this is a job you want. The only way to get immediate information, direct from the source's mouth and directly applicable to your own circumstance, is by asking questions.

*　*　*

Looking for work can be a frightening prospect. It seems that your whole future depends on one interview. When you're faced with difficult choices and are feeling pressure, you're likely to feel nervous as well; you don't ask as many questions as you should. Consequently you don't get the information you need.

This book is also meant to show how you can become a "questioning detective" and uncover the clues you need to locate the people who most want to hire you, tap into employers' true needs and concerns, sell yourself effectively in any interview situation, negotiate for more than money, and get the jobs you really want.

BUT WHAT DO I ASK?

Many times we don't ask questions because we're not sure what we should be asking. We figure interviewers are experts, they're the ones who do all the asking. So we don't speak up, and often come away from interviews with lingering doubts. We're not sure we presented ourselves to our best advantage. And often, we haven't found out enough about the job to determine if it's something we'd really like to do. "Was there something else I should have asked?" is the haunting refrain most of us have experienced after an interview.

You might wish you had an expert with you to get the necessary information. Well, now you have. This book will turn *you* into the expert. Write down the pertinent questions that apply to your situation. For example, if you want to let people know you're looking for a job, concentrate on the section about networking; if you're thinking of applying to an employment agency, study the questions in that section of the book.

In writing this book, I set out to explore some of the key issues that are on job seekers' minds. I tried to cover as many areas of interviewing as I could. There's no way I could address everyone's individual interviewing needs, but I tried to include the most important and frequently asked questions.

Every question opens up other questions. Add your own questions to the list. The questions here should get you started, and should stimulate your own questioning process so that you, too, can get the information you really need.

I don't claim to have exhausted all the questions you could, or should, ask about interviews. Nor do I intend to give you specific advice pertaining to your individual circumstances. I have provided questions and examples to give you a basis for comparison: I didn't want simply to provide you with a list of questions and let it go at that. I wanted you to understand why each of the questions is important, and what you should expect to learn from each answer.

THE HE/SHE ISSUE

One last word on a technical issue. I didn't want to include any gender bias in this book by constantly using "he" to refer to the interviewer. On the other hand, it is very awkward to use "he/she" and "him or her" throughout. So when referring to "the interviewer" or "the employer," I use "he" in some examples, and "she" in others.

This is your opportunity to be an active participant in one of the most important areas of your life. Most of us spend about 96,000 hours of our lives at work; we all want those hours to be fulfilling, satisfying, and challenging. You have the right to the kind of life you want and deserve. Make sure you stand up for that right, and start asking smart questions.

PART I

PLANNING AND PREPARATION

SMART QUESTIONS TO ASK ABOUT YOURSELF: TAKING THE ACTIVE ROAD TO JOB SUCCESS

Have you ever wished you could be cool, calm, and in control at interviews? Have you ever wanted to get the information you need to make a smart decision, find out what the boss was really looking for, and sell yourself into the job you've always wanted?

You can accomplish all of that by perfecting one simple technique you already know how to use—the fine art of asking questions. There are two reasons most people don't succeed at job interviews:

1. They are lacking in both the quantity and quality of the questions they ask.

2. They fail to see the whole picture—that a job search is made up of a *series* of question-and-answer interviews, and it's the entire process that gets you the job you want.

11

The skill of questioning is *the most important factor* in paving the road to interviewing success. With this skill you can handle any interview situation so that you will never have to ask yourself a question like, "How did I get myself into a job I hate so much?"

It is the linking of the art of questioning and the in-depth study of the various types of interviews that makes this book so special. This book will take you through the entire interviewing process—starting before you ever go on an interview and ending after you get the job. And every step of the way is paved with questions. Learn how to ask the right questions, and you'll get the answers you need.

Here is how most of us picture an interview situation:

We walk into a room and sit down facing an intimidating stranger across a large wooden desk. The interviewer (translate to: the interrogator) asks us a series of questions. We stutter and stammer our way through the answers, defending our lives and past work experiences. We are "dismissed" and await the final judgment.

That's how it feels, anyway. There is only one way to combat this feeling of terror, and that is to take control of the situation yourself. How do you do that? By asking questions of your own, by becoming a participant in the process rather than a victim of it.

Most of us think that the interviewing process begins when we sit down in front of a stranger and hope to make a good enough impression to be offered a job. To make that hope a reality, the process must begin way before that meeting ever takes place; there are several questions you must ask yourself before you go out on any type of interview.

There are also, of course, questions you must ask of others. What those questions are depends on the type of interview that's being conducted. Each type has a distinct character and purpose, and the types of questions you should be asking will be discussed in detail in later chapters.

However, one of the most important concepts you'll ever learn in the job-search process is to *get into the questioning habit*. It will build your confidence, give you that competitive edge, and allow you to take decisive action in the business of planning your life and your life's work.

Before you go on your next interview, ask yourself these smart questions:

- How much do I really know about myself and what I've accomplished?
- How much do I know about the kind of work I want to do, and the specific companies I want to work for?
- Do I know what employers are really looking for?
- Do I know how to go about getting the interviews I want?

Knowing the answers to each of these questions—in detail—will not only help you get a job, it will help you get the job you really want.

If you want to get a job—and get a job you want—there are two important steps you'll have to take:

SECRET STRATEGY NUMBER 1:
Become a questioning expert.

An interview is, by its very nature, a questioning process. You will be both asking and answering questions; the better you are at both of these, the better your chances of getting the results you want. We'll discuss more about actual questioning techniques in Section 7, but the commitment you make to the questioning process is more important than any technique you will learn.

You must become a questioning detective, seeking information every step of the way, until you "solve the case" and find the job that is just right for you.

SECRET STRATEGY NUMBER 2:
Learn to be *active, not reactive*.

There are many reasons the interview process is so misunderstood, but one of the greatest is the perception that this is a *passive* process. We see ourselves answering ads, sending out résumés, being called in for interviews, responding to a barrage of questions, and being either accepted or rejected. The reality is that getting a job hardly ever works this way, and certainly not in the midst of a recession.

You've got to change your attitude, paint a new picture, arouse your spirit of adventure. Realize that you will have to do your "homework" if you want to get interviews. You can't just sit back and wait for them to come to you.

LOADING UP YOUR ARSENAL OF ACCOMPLISHMENTS

I UNDERSTAND THE NEED FOR BEING ACTIVE, NOT REACTIVE. BUT HOW DO I BEGIN?

The first step is to take a good, hard look at yourself, find out who you really are, what it is you do well and enjoy doing, and just what it is that you have to offer prospective employers. This composite portrait of yourself is a tool you will use throughout your job-search process, and will add to continually for future use and reference. I call this tool an Arsenal of Accomplishments.

EXACTLY WHAT IS AN ARSENAL OF ACCOMPLISHMENTS?

An Arsenal of Accomplishments is a list of achievements you consider most satisfying and rewarding in your life. If you want to stand out in any interview situation, you have to be prepared to answer questions about yourself and your past accomplishments. Before you can do that, you must know what these accomplishments are.

You may think you already know, but I guarantee, unless you actually sit down and write a specific list, there are areas you will leave out. Most people come up with a very short list the first time around. This isn't due to a lack of accomplishments—it's because people often forget or undervalue their own achievements. Even if you do remember all your achievements right off, you have to know why these achievements were important. A prospective employer will want to know what effect your achievements had—on your company, your schoolwork, or your personal life.

I'VE ALREADY MADE UP MY RÉSUMÉ. ISN'T THAT ENOUGH?

A résumé tells you *what* you've done—and that's all. It doesn't tell you what that achievement meant to you or to the company for which you worked. You need this information for two reasons: the more you discover about your strengths, accomplishments and skills, the more confident you become about who you are and what you have to offer. And, the more you discover about yourself, the more you know about what it is that makes you *special*—what you can offer prospective employers that makes you stand out from the crowd.

WHAT IF I'M JUST GETTING OUT OF SCHOOL, OR DON'T HAVE A LOT OF WORK EXPERIENCE?

It doesn't matter if you have thirty years of work experience or if you have none. Everything you've done in your life—everything you are—counts.

Go back and look at your past with new eyes. Don't concentrate only on the "big" or the obvious. Look for the things that at first glance seem trivial or unimportant. Did you earn more merit badges than any other scout in your troop? Did you organize a soccer team for the kids in your neighborhood? Did you design a poster for your church's clothing drive? Taking stock of your accomplishments is an essential step to shining at interviews. This catalog is the ammunition you will use to shoot down any objections an interviewer might have about your ability to do the job; that's why it is called your Arsenal of Accomplishments.

HOW FAR BACK SHOULD I GO? WHAT SHOULD I INCLUDE?

Begin at the beginning. Take your time and think about various events in your life. Write them out in story form; they need not be in chronological order. They need not be job-related. If you're in school, think about how you've organized your study time, or were elected president of your class, or formed a chapter of Students Against Drunk Driving. If you have no work experience, think about how you've managed on a limited budget, organized a play group for neighborhood preschoolers, volunteered as a Big Brother to a less fortunate family, or stuck with a problem (and came up with a solution) when everyone else gave up trying.

If you currently have a job, think about how you saved

the company money or increased productivity, how you get along with coworkers and supervisors, how you developed new systems or improved old ones. Don't place value judgments on anything—just get it all down on paper.

Here are some guidelines to help you get started. Use these questions as springboards, then dive in and keep going on your own.

WHAT DID I ACCOMPLISH IN SCHOOL? (AREAS TO CONSIDER)

Courses:
   How were my grades? _____
   Did I get any special comments or commendations
      from teachers? _____
      _____
   What was my best subject? _____
   What made it special? _____
      _____

Clubs or Activities:
   Did I hold any offices? _____
      _____
   Was I part of any club competitions? _____
      _____
   Did I receive any awards or commendations? _____
      _____

Sports:
   What position did I play? _____
   How did I do in competition? _____
   Were there any outstanding games I remember? _____
      _____
   Any awards or commendations? _____
      _____

Part-time work:
How, when, and where? _____

_____

How did I balance job with schoolwork? _____

_____

What did I do with the money? _____

_____

Extracurricular activities? _____

_____

Community services? _____

_____

WHAT DID I ACCOMPLISH AT HOME? (AREAS TO CONSIDER)

Planning & Scheduling:
How did I run my day? _____

_____

How did I get things done for myself and my family?

_____

How did I keep track of schedules, appointments,
social events? _____

_____

Part-time work:
How, when, and where? _____

_____

How did I balance job with home duties? _____

_____

What did I do with the money? _____

_____

Volunteer work
How, when, and where? _____

_____

How did I balance job with home duties? _____
_____

Budgeting:
How do I keep my "books" or record my spending?
_____

How have I been able to save money for myself and
my family? _____
_____

How have I been able to make extra money? _____
_____

Prioritizing:
How do I decide what's most important in my day?
My week? Month? _____
_____
_____

Do I set goals for myself? _____
_____
_____

Do I accomplish them? _____
_____
_____

Hobbies and interests:
What are my special interests? _____
_____
_____

How do I spend my "spare" time? Do I read, travel,
cook, sew, write, work out, build furniture, sing,
etc.? _____
_____
_____

Other accomplishments: _____
_____

WHAT DID I ACCOMPLISH AT WORK? (AREAS TO CONSIDER)

Organization:
Have I set up systems to make my job (or my part of it) more efficient? _____

_____

How do I organize my day's work? _____

_____

How have I helped others be more organized? _____

_____

New ideas:
What new ideas have I had for my work or company?

_____

_____

Where did the ideas come from? _____

_____

How were they implemented? _____

_____

Saved company money:
What exactly did I do? _____

_____

How much money was involved? _____

_____

Was it an assigned task, or did I come up with the idea myself? _____
Was it a one-shot deal or a continuing assignment?

_____

Teamwork:
How do I get along with colleagues? _____

_____

With bosses and supervisors? _____

_____

Have I led any team projects? _____

_____

Been involved in any collaborative efforts? _____

_____

Affiliations, societies, associations:
What work-related organizations do I belong to? ____

_____

Do I participate or hold any office? _____

_____

Have I written for, or been featured in, the newsletter? _____

_____

Do I have any special responsibilities in the workplace (fire captain, CPR, etc.)? _____

_____

What does it involve? _____

_____

Other accomplishments: _____

_____

HUNTING DOWN YOUR HIDDEN SKILLS

Put aside your Arsenal of Accomplishments for a while. Did you notice any kind of pattern in your achievements? Do they show certain aptitudes or particular skills?

If you want to be able to sell yourself to prospective employers (which we'll discuss in detail in Section 4), you'll have to know which skills you possess. I'm not talking about technical expertise in a particular (and narrow) field. I'm talking about abilities that can be applied to whatever job you happen to be doing. These are your "salable" skills—skills that make you attractive to any "buyer"—and go with you from promotion to promotion, from company to company and even from one career to another.

WHAT EXACTLY IS A SKILL?

A skill is defined as anything you can learn to do competently, a developed aptitude or ability. Any of the skills on the list below can be taught, practiced, and mastered effectively. The more you use them, the easier they become. Go through the list and check off those items that apply to you:

Analyze and edit written material ____
Utilize library/research materials____
Conduct surveys and interviews____
Analyze and evaluate ideas and presentations____
Travel: meet with colleagues; meet with the public____
Identify problem areas ____
Develop new approaches to problems ____
Help people with their problems ____
Supervise and lead others ____
Evaluate and appraise others ____
Observe, inspect, review work of others ____
Plan, organize, systematize, revise ____
Work on long-term projects ____
Do detailed and accurate work ____
Meet work deadlines ____
Invent, imagine, create, design ____
Calculate, analyze, use computers ____
Motivate others ____
Be a team player____
Think logically ____
Manage time effectively ____

Manage stress effectively____
Set goals ____
Delegate ____
Teach or instruct ____
Coach ____
Think and act independently____
Be assertive when necessary____
Take risks when necessary ____
Ability and willingness to learn ____
Run effective meetings____
Adapt easily to new circumstances____

Here are some questions to ask yourself about the skills you've checked off:

DID I BREAK DOWN MY ACHIEVEMENT INTO ITS INDIVIDUAL STEPS, AND LIST THE SKILLS IN EACH STEP?

Suppose your achievement was that you found a new, less expensive printer for your company's updated brochure. What skills did that entail? You had to think logically, do extensive research, evaluate the quality of several vendors' work, negotiate with the vendors, analyze various bids, and write up your recommendations for your supervisors. That's quite an impressive list of skills! And though you may never have to perform this same task again, just imagine how you can put each of these skills to work in a wide variety of jobs.

DO I ENJOY USING THE SKILLS I'VE CHECKED OFF?

One of the skills you checked off in the example above was the ability to do research. You did it, but you disliked this phase of your job, and were anxious to get on to the "people" part of your assignment. It's good to know that you have research skills if you need them, but you wouldn't want to emphasize this skill too highly at an interview. Concentrate on skills that you do well and enjoy doing.

AM I BEING JUDGMENTAL, COMPARING MY SKILL LEVELS WITH OTHERS'?

You might be tempted to say, "All I did was find a new printer. George completely redesigned the company's brochure. He's much more creative than I am." First of all, finding ways to save money in this economy is *very* creative. Second, you can't compare your skills with anyone else's. Being good with numbers is *no better or worse* than being able to draw—they're two completely different skills and each is important in its own way.

HOW DO I USE MY ARSENAL OF ACCOMPLISHMENTS AND MY LIST OF SKILLS TO MY BEST ADVANTAGE?

The purpose of the Arsenal of Accomplishments and your list of hidden skills is to help you appreciate your true value. One of the most common situations you will run into is an interviewer who says, "Tell me about yourself." What are you going to say? Are you going to tell your whole life story? Not a good idea. You have to be selective.

Go back to your Arsenal of Accomplishments and find the first one listed. You are now going to divide it into distinct sections that answer three powerful questions:

Why?

How?

What?

Let's take our earlier example of finding a new printer.

Why did you do what you did? You needed to find a less expensive way of producing the company's brochure.

How did you solve the problem? You researched vendors in your area, analyzed which vendors could supply both high quality and acceptable price, and negotiated the best deals.

What actually happened due to the actions you took? You saved your company $9,500 in printing costs.

Continue on with your own list.

BLOWING YOUR OWN HORN

You're creating this list of Whys, Hows, and Whats for two important reasons. One is to enable you to include one or two in your cover letter to prospective employers so that they will grant you an interview. The second is so that you can realize, and appreciate, all the things you have accomplished so far in your life—and can communicate these accomplishments to those people who will need and value your special skills.

SECRET STRATEGY NUMBER 3:
Be your own PR firm.

IS A JOB SEARCH REALLY LIKE A PUBLIC-RELATIONS CAMPAIGN?

People hire public-relations firms to help them get the word out about themselves, their product, or their service. The object is to make customers aware of their existence. You want to make your customers, or prospective interviewers, aware of your existence. It would be great if you could hire a public-relations firm to help you get the word out, but since that is neither practical nor desirable, you must act as your own PR agent.

HOW DO I START MY CAMPAIGN?

A public-relations firm would start by asking you all the questions you've just asked yourself, then distill all this information into a press release that they would send out to appropriate parties.

Since you are your own PR firm, you must distill all the information you just gained about yourself, and use it to promote yourself to potential buyers. These are the elements of your public-relations campaign:

- You're building a network of contacts.
- You're demonstrating your "product's" most attractive, and salable, features.
- You're getting the word out that you have a terrific product available on the market right now.
- You're putting together "press releases"—your cover letters, résumé, and any other correspondence relating to your job search are the first materials your "buyers" will see—so make them work for you.

SOME PUBLIC-RELATIONS FIRMS HAVE THE REPUTATION— DESERVED OR NOT—OF USING "HYPE" OR EXAGGERATION IN THEIR CAMPAIGNS. WILL THIS BE PART OF MY CAMPAIGN AS WELL?

No, it will not. You're simply going to use what you've discovered about yourself to let others know what you have to offer. And you're going to show yourself in the best possible light. Always tell the truth—but make it short, sweet, and punchy. Focus on your accomplishments, and the results they achieved.

WHAT'S THE BEST WAY TO MAKE MY ACCOMPLISHMENTS "SHORT, SWEET, AND PUNCHY"?

Use dynamic words and strong action verbs. Don't say "I worked on this program." It's much better to say, "I implemented (or organized) this project." It's better to say "I analyzed" rather than "I saw," or "I designed and created" rather than "I wrote" or "I did." Use a good dictionary and thesaurus and discover the most potent action verbs possible.

IS THERE ANYTHING SPECIAL I SHOULD CONCENTRATE ON? ANYTHING THAT EMPLOYERS ARE MOST INTERESTED IN KNOWING?

Any company that hires you is making an investment in you—an investment in time and money. Like any smart investor, the company will want to know just how good an investment it's making. *Potential employers are, therefore, always interested in the bottom line.* Whenever possible, try to show your accomplishments in dollars or percentages. It demonstrates your business sense and your concern for costs and expenses. Did you ever increase your company's profits? Decrease costs? Increase sales or productivity? Put it all down in writing.

HOW DO I KNOW (OR FIND OUT) HOW MUCH I CONTRIBUTED?

As employees we all have an impact, directly or indirectly. Find out how your efforts connect to the bottom line. If possible, set up a system of measurement with the financial people in your company.

Don't wait until tomorrow to start connecting each assignment, each task and project to your company's gross profits. In jobs like public relations, advertising, training, and administration, it may be more difficult—but become a detective and find that connection.

Wendy, a buyer in a department store, got a great deal on an up-and-coming designer's new line of sweaters. The sweaters became so popular, the store created a separate department for this designer's clothes. Wendy discovered that the new designer's department had improved the company's bottom line by $420,000. When she started looking for a new job, Wendy was able to use this figure to impress interviewers with the fact that she was so instrumental in increasing the company's profits.

This extra effort, this targeted probing, can make all the difference between an average interview and one that gets you the job offer you want.

PRIORITIZING YOUR CONCERNS

If you were going to buy a car, you'd do a lot of research because it is an important decision and a large expenditure. You'd probably read consumer magazines, study mileage comparisons, research safety features, and get price quotes. All of these things are extremely important, and they are important to everyone who buys a car. But in addition to all this research, you've probably already made a mental list of all the things that are most important to *you*—features that are either highly desirable or absolutely necessary for your car to have.

Your list might include: four doors, extra safety features, child-proof locks and windows, lots of trunk room, dark blue. Another person's list might include: all leather interior, great sound system, four-wheel drive, bright red. Obviously, the priorities for these two people are vastly different.

When you're doing your research, the same principles apply. There are "standard" features about most jobs that everyone wants to know: the size of the company, the salary for the job, the job responsibilities, etc. But until you've developed you own personal job priority list, you won't be able to make a decision that's in your best interest.

HOW DO I MAKE MY OWN PERSONAL PRIORITY LIST?

What are the "features" of a job that are most important to you at this time? Your list might include such items as:

> My own computer
> No more than forty-five minutes travel time
> Limited business trips
> Handicapped accessibility
> Pension plan
> Health insurance
> Large company with lots of people contact

Make a list of your own, including both the features you *want* and the features you *need*. Now go back through your list and divide it into two sections. In one column, place those items that are absolute requirements. If you were in a wheelchair, for instance, you could not work in a company that was not accessible to the handicapped. Limited business trips might also be a requirement for you. You might be willing to work for a company that is one hour away, or to work for a smaller company than you had originally envisioned. These items would go in the second column, which is reserved for those features on which you will be willing to compromise, or even forgo. Your new list might look like this:

Required Features	Desirable Features
Handicap accessibility	45-minute commute
Limited business trips	Own computer
Child care	Size of company
Pension plan	
Health insurance	

Make your own personal priority list:

_____

_____

_____

_____

_____

_____

_____

_____

_____

_____

_____

_____

_____

_____

_____

_____

_____

Now divide your list into required and desirable features:

REQUIRED FEATURES	DESIRABLE FEATURES

Once you have this list, and have divided it accordingly, you can go into any interview situation and know what is most important to you in a job. You'll know that you have to ask about pension plans and health insurance before you can accept a job. You'll know that you would like to have your own computer at work, but that you would be willing to share access if necessary.

You don't necessarily have to wait until you are face-to-face with a prospective boss to ask these questions. Personnel may be able to tell you about pensions and health insurance, for instance. An employment agency or headhunter should be able to give you information about the size of the company, and a general idea of how it is structured.

SECRET STRATEGY NUMBER 4:
Make, and memorize, your personal priority list.

*   *   *

You have just completed the first, and most important, phase of interviewing success—knowing yourself and what you're looking for. Because you now have a thorough knowledge of yourself and your background, you won't feel put on the spot trying to come up with impressive stories. Imagine that an interviewer says, "I'm looking for someone who can help us find ways to keep costs down. Can you tell me something about yourself that would demonstrate your abilities in that area?" If you hadn't done your detective work, you might not have remembered your most impressive story. You wouldn't have had anything to offer as proof of your abilities. But because you've done your homework, the question doesn't take you by surprise; you have a good answer and you make a good impression.

Knowing what you're looking for is more important these days than ever before. Once you get a job, you're going to want to keep it. Therefore, you don't want to accept a job just because it is offered to you. You want to go after interviews for positions that meet most of your criteria. There's nothing worse than being stuck in a job that makes you miserable and feeling there's no way out. Knowing what you *want* and *need* from the jobs you pursue will help you focus and have more control over the entire job-search process.

It's time to move on to the next area of knowledge you'll need to shine at any interview—what you need to know about the people, and the companies, for whom you wish to work.

SECTION 2

SMART QUESTIONS TO ASK ABOUT THE JOB MARKET: GETTING THE INSIDE STORY

How does having information about a prospective employer and/or the company for which you want to work help you in an interview situation? There are actually a number of reasons. Perhaps the most important, however, is that it lets the interviewer know you take this opportunity seriously, and are sincerely interested in working for this particular company.

Just for a moment, put yourself in a boss's position. Imagine that it is your responsibility to hire a new assistant marketing director. You are interviewing two candidates today. They both graduated from prestigious colleges, they both have five years of experience working for reputable companies. You have a pleasant interview with Candidate A. After twenty minutes or so you say, "Do you have any questions for me?"

Candidate A replies, "What exactly does your company do?"

After twenty minutes of talking to Candidate B, you ask again, "Do you have any questions for me?" Candidate B replies, "I read in a trade journal last week that Brad Johnson is coming in as the new CEO in September. How do you think that will affect the company's marketing strategies?"

Which candidate would you hire? Of course you would choose Candidate B. By that one question, you can tell that this is a person who 1) keeps up on industry developments by reading trade journals; 2) took the time and effort to find out what was happening in this company; 3) was able to digest the information and come up with an intelligent, relevant question; and 4) prepared specifically for *this* interview, letting you know that this specific job, and this employer, are of great importance. If this candidate took this kind of time and effort to prepare for the interview, it's likely that this is a person who will put the same kind of time and effort into the job.

Your choice probably had little to do with where the "applicants" went to school, or whether or not they had perfect résumés. Your choice was more likely based on which person knew more about you, and about what it might take to do a good job as your personal assistant.

ARE THERE OTHER REASONS THIS KIND OF RESEARCH MIGHT PAY OFF IN THE END?

Convincing a boss that you are the right person for the job isn't the only reason you need to do research. There are at least three other reasons for gathering knowledge about the companies you want to work for:

1. To get vital information about the types of jobs

and/or industries in which you are interested—including educational and skill requirements, economic factors, stress levels, etc.
2. To discover options and help you make decisions about where, when, and for whom you would like to work.
3. To discover exactly who at those companies has the authority to hire you, to find out how to set up interviews with those people, and if at all possible, to find out what the prospective bosses are like.

People often object to the amount of time it takes to do this kind of research. But think of the time that will be wasted going on dozens of interviews for jobs in fields that don't really interest you!

SECRET STRATEGY NUMBER 5:
Research prospective companies to help you
focus on getting the job you really want.

WHAT'S SO IMPORTANT ABOUT HAVING A FOCUS?

Without focus, you won't know where to begin to look for a job. It's like saying, "I want to work in California." That's a pretty vague goal. Is there some particular area of California in which you'd be happiest? Isn't there some particular job you'd like to do? You can spend your life answering help-wanted ads from every newspaper for every available position. Or you can do your research, discover what companies in which parts of the country suit your skills and interests, and focus your efforts on getting interviews in those areas.

The point is, you don't want to find just any job—you

want to find the job that is right for you. And once you find out about that job, you want to have the competitive edge. You want to be sure the interviewer knows you're the right person for that job. In order to make that happen, you have to put in the effort and do the research.

THE BIG PICTURE: RESEARCHING THE INDUSTRY

Before you can begin to do research on specific companies, take a look at the overall area in which you're interested. This will give you an idea of the kinds of jobs available throughout the industry, not just within one company. If you're interested in the law, for example, an overview of the industry will tell you that there are hundreds of specialty areas in which you could conceivably practice. There are firms that specialize in criminal cases, in environmental law, in copyright law, or in corporate law, just to name a few. Studying the industry as a whole will give you a better idea of what's out there, and provide you with options you may never have known existed.

WHAT'S THE BEST WAY TO GET INFORMATION ON THE INDUSTRY IN WHICH I'M INTERESTED?

Go on information interviews, where you get "insider information" from those already in the field (discussed in detail in Section 10). Read, read, read. Find out what trade papers or magazines carry information about this industry. If you don't know what you should be reading, use the *Encyclopedia of Associations*. It lists thousands of trade and professional associations. Call up the appropriate association and ask which journals are the best in their industry. Or use the *Reader's Guide to Periodical Literature* or the *Business Periodicals Index* to find articles relevant to your industry.

WHAT ARE THE QUESTIONS I SHOULD BE ASKING WHEN DOING RESEARCH ABOUT AN INDUSTRY?

Use the worksheet below to help your research efforts. Add any other questions relevant to the particular industry in which you're interested.

Which are the dominant firms in this industry?

_____

_____

Is there one industry leader, several large companies, or smaller firms scattered about the country (or any combination of the above)? _____

_____

Is this industry located in a particular geographical area? In one part of the country? In large cities? In rural areas? _____

_____

What is the current status of this industry? Is it long-established and financially sound? Is it up-and-coming and growth oriented?_____

_____

Are there technical advances that are affecting this industry? _____

_____

_____

Are the products and/or services of this industry in demand? _____

_____

Is it a "hot" field? If so, will it stay hot? _____

_____

Is there controversy surrounding this industry? If so, what is it? _____

_____

Is it at all concerned with issues such as pollution, community involvement, public service?

_____

_____

What are the professional organizations and associations in this industry? _____

_____

Do the associations have job placement services?

_____

What kind of educational or vocational training do you need in this industry? _____

_____

_____

WHAT RESEARCH SOURCES ARE AVAILABLE TO STUDY PARTICULAR INDUSTRIES?

Some sources (most of which are available in the reference section of the library) to help you find out about particular industries include:

- Directory of Professional and Trade Organizations
- Dun & Bradstreet's Middle Market Directory
- Dun & Bradstreet's Million Dollar Directory
- Dun & Bradstreet's Billion Dollar Directory
- Occupational Outlook Handbook (U.S. Dept. of Labor)
- Standard & Poor's Industrial Index
- Standard & Poor's Stock Buyer's Compendium of American Industry
- Standard Rate and Data Business Publications Directory

IS ANY OF THIS INFORMATION AVAILABLE ON COMPUTER DATA BASES?

Yes, some of which include:

- Economic Information Systems Industrial Plants (EIS Industrial). Economic Information Systems, Control Data Corporation, New York, NY.
- Predicasts Overview of Markets and Technology (PTSPROMT). Predicasts, Cleveland, OH.
- Standard & Poor's News. Standard & Poor's, New York, NY.

GETTING MORE SPECIFIC: RESEARCHING INDIVIDUAL COMPANIES

Now that you've become an expert in the industry of your choice, it's time to get down to specifics. You need to narrow and refine your research. You want to find out everything possible about specific companies, and about individuals at these companies who might be in a position to interview and hire you.

Use the worksheet below to help your research:

Do I know exactly what this company makes, sells, or provides for its customers?_____

_____

How large (or small) is the organization? _____

_____

Do I know anything about the internal structure of this company? Do I know who heads the company, and how the hierarchical structure works—how many vice-presidents, assistant vice-presidents, managers, etc.?

_____

_____

_____

_____

How is the company organized (who reports to whom)? _____

_____

_____

Is it a family-owned, privately, or publicly held company?

_____

Is it an old, established firm, or a new, growth-oriented company? _____

_____

Do I know anything about the financial soundness of this company? _____

_____

What is its reputation in the industry? In the community?
_____
_____

Have there been any radical changes in ownership or management recently? _____
_____
_____

Is there more than one branch of the company? If so, where?
_____
_____

Does the company promote from within? _____

Are there women and minorities in high-level management positions?_____
_____

Who at this company is the person responsible for hiring someone to fill the position I'm seeking?
_____
_____

Have I found out enough about this company to know whether or not I'd like to work there? _____
_____

WHAT'S THE BEST WAY TO GET INFORMATION ABOUT A COMPANY?

If at all possible, try to get information from people who work at the company. Ask friends and relatives if they know anyone who works (or worked) there. It's always best to get an insider's view of the daily life of an organization. Find out as much as you can about the company's style: Is it formal? Casual? High pressure? Low-key? Is there a supportive atmosphere, or are there a lot of unpleasant office politics? Are there opportunities for advancement? Is your "insider" happy there? The more you can find out before you go into an interview, the better your chances at making a good impression.

IS THERE ANY WAY I CAN GET A FIRSTHAND IMPRESSION OF THE COMPANY?

If you're in close proximity to the company, take a look at it for yourself. If you're considering a job with the corporate headquarters of a large retail chain, for instance, visit one of the stores. How does it strike you? Were you treated well? Did the employees seem bored? Happy? Hostile?

If it's not a place you can visit, try calling the main office for some easy information, such as the spelling of someone's name or the company's mailing address. What is the receptionist's attitude? Is she polite? If she's rude and harried, it's a good indication that there's a company-wide problem. It shows that customer relations are not a high priority for this company—and that is a serious offense in these tough economic times. It also shows that the company doesn't care enough to train its employees properly.

How much a company cares is part of its corporate culture. Companies have personalities just like people do: your personality must be compatible with theirs; otherwise the relationship will never work. Some companies are extremely conservative and traditional; others are more aggressive and experimental. If you enjoy a more aggressive, innovative atmosphere, you probably won't be happy in a staid, conservative corporation. If you can make a personal visit to the company and see just what the atmosphere is really like, it may help you make a decision as to whether or not you'd like to work there.

ARE THERE ANY TYPES OF INTERVIEWS I CAN USE AS RESEARCH SOURCES?

Yes, there are. You can use information and networking interviews (explained in detail in later sections). You may want to arrange an interview with someone in the company who has nothing to do with the hiring process. That way you will probably feel freer to ask questions about the internal workings of the company, and the interviewer will probably be more open with his answers. If you can't arrange to speak to someone in the company, use your networking skills to find someone involved in the industry, and familiar with this company.

IS THERE ANY INFORMATION I CAN GET DIRECTLY FROM THE COMPANY?

You may want to look at the company's annual report. Call the company directly and ask them to send it to you. Be sure to read the annual report thoroughly. Read any footnotes in the report, as they often contain valuable information. Read the profiles of the top executives. Study their photos. This should give you a clue as to the general personality type the company prefers to hire.

A few notes about annual reports, however. You should not rely on an annual report as the sole criterion for a company. After all, the company (or its PR department) creates the report so that the company is shown in a favorable light. Be sure you use other sources before you decide whether or not to pursue interviews at a particular company.

ARE TRADE JOURNALS AND PROFESSIONAL PUBLICATIONS GOOD RESEARCH SOURCES?

They are very good sources of information on the industry as a whole. Also, they often contain articles on individual companies and interesting executives at these companies. These publications usually have help-wanted ads as well. And don't forget to check out which companies are advertising in these journals. They may be leads to other interview opportunities.

WHAT ABOUT DIRECTORIES AND REFERENCE BOOKS?

You'll find valuable information in:

- The Directory of Leading Private Companies
- Dun's Employment Opportunity Directory/The Career Guide
- The Fortune Directory of U.S. Corporations
- Moody's Complete Corporate Index
- Poor's Register of Corporations, Directors and Executives
- Thomas' Register
- Who's Who in America
- Who's Who of American Women

Another valuable guide is *How to Get Information About Companies,* available from Washington Researchers Publishers, Washington, DC.

ARE ANY OF THESE RESOURCES AVAILABLE ON COMPUTER DATA BASES?

Yes, there are some, including:

- Abstracted Business Information (ABI/INFORM). Data Courier, Louisville, KY.
- Compustat II Data Bank. Standard & Poor's Compustat, Englewood, CO.
- D&B Financial Profile. Dun & Bradstreet, New York, NY.
- LC/LINE. System Development Corporation, Santa Monica, CA.
- Nexis Data Base (NEXIS). Mead Data Central, Miamisburg, OH.

GETTING MOST SPECIFIC: RESEARCHING INDIVIDUAL EMPLOYERS

This is perhaps the most difficult area to research, and information may not always be available to you. However, if it is at all possible, you want to find out as much information as you can about the individuals who may be hiring you.

ARE THERE RESOURCES AVAILABLE THAT WILL PROVIDE INFORMATION ON INDIVIDUALS WITHIN A COMPANY?

Many of the resources listed previously in this chapter include brief profiles of top officers and executives. Annual reports from individual companies often include lengthy bios of their executive officers.

Newspapers and magazines are also good sources of information about larger companies' executive officers. Many libraries now have computer data bases available that make it easy to enter an individual's name and receive a list of articles recently published about that person.

These high-level officers may not be the people with whom you would have direct contact. However, information about them will give you a good idea of the corporate culture and style they generate. A conservative, old-line CEO, for example, probably runs a conservative company. A more aggressive risk-taker most likely runs a faster-paced, more aggressive organization.

I'M INTERESTED IN WORKING FOR SMALLER FIRMS THAT AREN'T LISTED IN THESE RESOURCE GUIDES. HOW CAN I GET INFORMATION ON INDIVIDUALS IN THOSE COMPANIES?

In this case, you may have to change your detective work to a more personal style. (This also applies if you want to get information about middle- or lower-level managers in larger companies.)

Your best bet, once again, is to try to find someone who works (or has worked) at that company. You want to get an insider's opinion and evaluation. Find out if that insider knows the person with whom you'd like to get an interview. If they do, ask for information. What is this person like as a boss? What is her management style? Does she have any interesting hobbies that they know about? The more you know about an individual employer before the interview, the easier it will be to establish a rapport and tune into her needs.

WHAT IF I DON'T KNOW ANYONE WHO WORKS AT THE COMPANY. ARE THERE OTHER WAYS TO GET INFORMATION?

Perhaps. When you get to the point of actually calling to set up an interview appointment, you may be able to get information from the secretary or receptionist. You don't want to be too pushy, or appear to be prying into the interviewer's private life. But if you've established a good rapport with the secretary (see Section 16), a question such as, "What kind of interview can I expect with Mr. Smith?" may provide you with valuable insight and information about the boss's style and personality.

In the first chapter, you became reacquainted with yourself so that you have a list of accomplishments you can use effectively in any interview. In this chapter, you learned what you need to know about the industries, companies, and individuals with whom you'll be seeking interviews.

In the next chapter you'll learn more about how bosses *really* think—and what they're hoping to find each time they interview a prospective employee.

SECTION 3

SMART QUESTIONS TO ASK ABOUT EMPLOYERS: WHAT ARE THEY REALLY LOOKING FOR

You are the most important resource a company can have, the most important investment it will make. Each hiring decision costs a company time and money—and a wrong decision can lose clients, hurt morale, and damage public image. So if you want a job with challenge and opportunity, you will have to prove to an interviewer that you know what it takes to be the kind of employee bosses want to hire. And you'll have to prove to a potential boss that he or she is making the right decision by hiring you.

Every job has particular skill requirements. Engineers, chemists, technicians, researchers, teachers, editors, salespeople, doctors, lawyers, investment bankers—whatever profession you pursue has specific educational and training prerequisites. Assuming you have the needed skills, what will make an interviewer want to send you on to the next interview, or make a boss want to hire you rather than the next person with the same education, training, and experience?

THINK LIKE A BOSS

HOW DO I KNOW WHAT TODAY'S EMPLOYERS ARE REALLY LOOKING FOR? WHAT THEY REALLY WANT?

There's only one way you can find out the answers to these questions, and that is by remembering this Secret Strategy:

SECRET STRATEGY NUMBER 6:
Think like a boss!

Norman Vincent Peale, the father of positive thinking, told me this story about a young man who followed this credo. This young man read an ad in the paper that said, "College grads appear 8:30 Saturday morning for a job interview." The young man desperately needed a job, so he got up, got dressed, and went to the address forty-five minutes early, thinking he'd be first on line. To his chagrin, there were twenty other applicants ahead of him. But he wasn't discouraged for long. He took out a piece of paper and wrote a few words. He handed the paper to the receptionist and asked her to bring it in to the boss, who looked at it and read, "I'm the twenty-first guy on line. Don't do a thing until you see me." The young man had the right attitude, and he got the job.

WHAT MADE THIS JOB SEEKER SO SUCCESSFUL?

It's because he knew how to *think like a boss*. Standing

on line, he thought to himself, "What would make a boss want to see number twenty-one on line?" Just sending in another résumé, one probably very similar to the other twenty ahead of his, wouldn't do it. He figured the boss would appreciate someone with initiative, someone willing to take a chance, someone with a sense of humor. And he was right! He thought about what he would pay attention to if he were in the boss's place, and then acted accordingly.

DOES THAT MEAN I'M SUPPOSED TO PRETEND TO BE THE BOSS?

No, it means that you should try to put yourself in the boss's shoes. Do what successful salespeople do—empathize. When you go in for an interview, you are a salesperson—you're selling yourself to the prospective employer. The boss is your customer; he's the one who will be buying your services. What you need to do in every interview is to make the interviewer feel that she is special, and that you care about what you can do for her, not just what she can do for you.

WHAT EXACTLY AM I SELLING? MY SKILLS AND EXPERIENCE?

You are selling your skills and experience, but you're doing more than that. You are embarking on a marketing campaign.

Marketing is the ability to fill a need—NOT YOUR NEEDS, but your potential buyer, or employer's, needs. And bosses have a lot of needs—they need you to fill the requirements of the job in terms of skill and experience, but they also have *emotional needs* they are looking to fill.

When a boss hires you, she is purchasing your services for her company. Making a purchase—any purchase—is an *emotional decision, not a logical one*. Think about your own shopping experiences. Suppose, once again, you need a car. You make out a list of requirements this car needs to fulfill: it needs to get good mileage, it needs to hold at least five people because you're in a car pool, it needs to be within a certain price range. These are logical, practical considerations. But why do you choose one particular model or color over another? Perhaps because it's like your best friend's car, or perhaps it's because red makes you feel powerful. In the end, your final decision about which car to buy is based on your *emotional* criteria.

IS HIRING A NEW EMPLOYEE AN EMOTIONAL DECISION AS WELL?

All hiring choices are ultimately based on the boss's emotional criteria. Your job is to find out what those emotional needs are, and to let him know that you have the ability to fill them.

Now I want you to imagine yourself a boss. If you've been in a managerial position, this will be easy for you. Think about interviews you've conducted in the past—what went well, and what didn't. Who would your ideal candidate have been? If you haven't been in a managerial position, I want you to learn to think, *and feel,* like a boss. What would you do first if you had to hire a new employee? You'd probably sit in your office and fantasize about the perfect employee. You want someone who will relieve you of your worries, someone who is dependable, creative, and supportive.

You want someone who will fit in with the rest of the team, someone who is friendly, willing to pitch in, willing to listen to suggestions and to be flexible in changing situations. You want someone who will care about the company and care about you, someone you feel comfortable with, someone to whom you can relate, someone you like.

You've been burned many times in the past. You've been let down by people who never show up, who show up late, who rush out the door at exactly five o'clock, who quit without notice. This time you want to hire someone who cares about you and your problems.

Picturing yourself in the boss's position, you can see why skills and experience sometimes take a backseat to other, more personal characteristics.

TEN SUCCESS FACTORS

As I wrote in my book *Marketing Yourself,* today's employers are screening candidates for more than their skills and experience. They are looking for the "success factors"—those personal characteristics that are not specific to one industry, job, or career, but that will bring you success in *any* job or career.

WHAT ARE SOME OF THE PERSONAL CHARACTERISTICS THAT EMPLOYERS ADMIRE?

The success factors most sought after by employers include:

Adaptability: Adaptability is the ability to adjust yourself easily and willingly to different conditions, and to see change as a challenge and an opportunity. Before you go on any interview, ask yourself: Which of my accomplishments best demonstrates my adaptability?

_____

_____

_____

Commitment: Although you may not be able to promise you will stay with a particular company for twenty years, you must be committed to doing the job at hand and giving it your best. Show yourself to be a reliable, responsible person. Before you go on any interview, ask yourself: Which of my accomplishments best demonstrates my commitment?

_____

_____

_____

Communication: We are now in the age of the service society, and how we communicate with those around us often determines our level of success. Everything about you is related to communications: the letters you send, the phone calls you make, your appearance, your attitude. Before you go on any interview, ask yourself: Which of my accomplishments best demonstrates my communications skills?

_____

_____

_____

Creativity: Creativity is really about different ways of looking at things. It begins with taking an objective look at a problem or obstacle, and combining imagination and reason to discover a solution. Employers are always on the lookout for creative problem solvers. Before you go on any interview, ask yourself: Which of my accomplishments best demonstrates my creativity?

_____

_____

_____

Decision Making: People at all levels of work are being asked to make more and more decisions. As there is more information available to each of us than ever before, the need for confident decision-making abilities is stronger than ever before. Before you go on any interview, ask yourself: Which of my accomplishments best demonstrates my decision-making ability?

_____

_____

_____

Evaluation: How well are you able to handle a work-related crisis? Do you panic and fall apart? Or are you able to look at a work load, set priorities, and find ways to solve the most immediate problems? Obviously, employers are looking for people who fit into the latter category. The ability to make reasonable judgments and assess unexpected situations is of great value on any job. Before you go on any interview, ask yourself: Which of my accomplishments best demonstrates my evaluation ability?

_____

_____

_____

Foresight: Foresight comes from a careful analysis of present conditions, along with a realistic projection of future trends. All employers are looking for people with foresight, go-getters who can think in terms of expanding their markets, creating new applications for established products, or finding variations on services now provided. If you can demonstrate to an employer that you accomplished any of these in the past, it will be a strong selling point in your favor. Before you go on any interview, ask yourself: Which of my accomplishments best demonstrates my foresight?

_____

_____

_____

Independence: The ability to work on your own is becoming more and more important, whether you work as a free-lancer or as a part of a large corporation. Employers want to know that you will be able to take a project and get it done without having to be told what to do every step of the way. Before you go on any interview, ask yourself: Which of my accomplishments best demonstrates my independence?

_____

_____

_____

Team Player: Independence must be tempered with the ability to work with others. The best teams are those that respect and use the talents of all their players. Each team member has his or her own job to do—but each player also knows that winning depends on everyone working together. Be sure to let employers know about accomplishments that required you to work as part of a team. Before you go on any interview, ask yourself: Which of my accomplishments best demonstrates my ability to be a team player?

_____

_____

_____

Value-Added Marketing: With more and more people in business today having direct contact with the public, every employee becomes a customer-service representative. This is leading employers to hire people who go beyond what is absolutely necessary to get the job done. Employers want people to give more than what's expected—to the company, to the customer, and to themselves. Before you go on any interview, ask yourself: Which of my accomplishments best demonstrates my commitment to value-added marketing?

_____

_____

_____

HOW CAN I CONVINCE AN EMPLOYER THAT I HAVE THESE SUCCESS FACTORS, THAT I HAVE WHAT SHE'S LOOKING FOR?

When an interviewer asks about past accomplishments, most people simply list their achievements as if they were reciting their résumé. However, you can't come out and say, "Hire me. I'm adaptable, committed, independent, and a team player." If you want to make an impact, you have to show the employer how your past relates to her future.

Suppose you went to an interview at Widgets Inc. and the boss said, "I see you graduated from the University of Florida. What did you study there?" You could just say, "I majored in economics."

If you were the boss, what would you be thinking in response to that answer? You'd be thinking, "SO WHAT?" You have to fill in the "so what" for her. Finish your answer by saying, "As a matter of fact, I did my term paper on widgets and their impact on our economy.

That's why I want to work here at Widgets Inc.—because I know how far widgets can go, and I want to be part of the team to help take them there." Hidden in this answer are clues to your independence, your foresight, and your value-added marketing.

You've got to make the connection between what you have to offer and the employer's emotional needs. You've got to let the employer know how hiring you will make his life easier.

IF I'M GOING TO THINK LIKE A BOSS, I NEED TO KNOW HOW BOSSES VIEW THE HIRING SITUATION. WHAT'S AT STAKE FOR THEM?

Bosses have a lot at stake when they make a hiring decision. Most people go to a job interview thinking they are the underdog; that the prospective boss is cool, calm, collected, and in control. Nothing could be further from the truth. Bosses are nervous! The company could lose anywhere from $7,000 to $12,000 for every poor hiring decision, and bosses who make poor hiring decisions can lose their own jobs.

Bosses hate hiring! They hate hiring almost as much as you hate job hunting! They will do anything to avoid the grueling, risky, and time-consuming hiring process. They're desperately hoping that you will be the one who can help them out of the bind they're in. But what do most job seekers do? They go into an interview as if they are saying, "HELP ME! EMPLOY ME! I NEED A JOB!"

What they should be saying is, "What do you need? How can I help you?" It is not easy being a boss. If you can think like a boss and make a prospective employer feel that you care about this job, that you will make his life easier, if you can convince the employer that you have what he is really looking for, then you'll get a job offer every time.

COMMUNICATING RIGHT FROM THE START

Bosses want to hire people who will make them look good to *their* bosses; therefore they are looking for people who can communicate, who can speak well for themselves, who can write effective letters, who have energy and enthusiasm.

You must communicate this energy and enthusiasm in every interview you go on—whether you're networking, getting information, talking to the boss's secretary, or facing the boss one-on-one.

I'VE BEEN TOLD THAT MY TELEPHONE VOICE IS SOMEWHAT GRATING. SINCE I'M NOT APPLYING FOR JOBS AS A TELE-MARKETER OR RECEPTIONIST, WILL THAT HURT MY CHANCES OF GETTING HIRED?

It's possible. Often the first contact you have with a potential interviewer is over the phone. Since the interviewer can't see you, he is going to judge you by how you sound. Your voice can be a help or a liability—it can give you away as being shy and nervous, or convey the impression of healthy self-confidence.

When I was looking for a part-time assistant for my office, I did a lot of preliminary interviewing over the phone. Since the person I was looking for would be required to answer the phone, voice quality was a critical factor in my decision. The first day two women called. They both seemed nice and intelligent and could easily handle the tasks I had in mind for this position. But the second woman who called had very little energy in her voice. I had to ask her to speak up twice. I liked what she had to say, and I'm sure she could have done the job, but I couldn't hire her because of the quality of her voice.

HOW IMPORTANT IS MY PHYSICAL APPEARANCE TO AN INTERVIEW?

Millions of dollars are spent every year by marketing experts on design and packaging. You don't have to spend millions of dollars on your own packaging, but you should be aware of the overall impression you make. When you go into an interview, are you aware of the impression you make, physically and verbally?

If you walk into an interview with your hair in your eyes, your clothes all askew, and your shoulders scrunched up to your ears, you'll have to work very hard to get the employer to see beyond the "packaging."

Make a checklist for yourself to use before every interview, such as:

___Is my hair neat and clean?
___Are my clothes pressed, and appropriate for this company?
___Have I worked on my voice and my diction?
___Have I practiced a firm, steady handshake?
___Am I aware of any nervous habits to avoid during the interview?
___Does my overall "package" convey the image of a hardworking, reliable professional?
___Can I communicate to a potential boss why making a decision to hire me would be the right decision to make?

Believe it or not, the prospective boss is rooting for you. She wants to end the job search; she wants you to be the answer to her problems. Go into an interview with empathy and understanding of the boss's position. Reassure her that you are the best person for the job. How do you do that? As you'll see in the next chapter, by seeing—and selling—yourself from the boss's perspective.

SECTION 4

SMART QUESTIONS TO ASK ABOUT WHY EMPLOYERS "BUY": SEEING (AND SELLING) YOURSELF FROM THE INTERVIEWER'S PERSPECTIVE

What is the main reason that you buy any product?

The *only* reason you buy anything—from a box of paper clips to a yacht—is because *there's something in it for you*. You don't buy paper clips just because they hold your papers together. You buy them because they make you feel organized, they make you feel professional. You don't buy a yacht because you need a boat. You buy a yacht because it makes you feel powerful and gives you a feeling of status and superiority. You buy to fulfill your emotional needs.

As we said in the last chapter, interviewers "buy" your product—you—if you fulfill their emotional needs. In this case, however, you are not only the product, you are the salesperson as well. And the most successful sales-

61

people rely on what is known in the sales trade as *benefit selling*, based on the principle that all customers are asking themselves one simple question before they buy anything: "What's in it for me?"

WHY PEOPLE BUY

The definition of selling is simply showing someone else how your product or service will help him or her fill a need or solve a problem. That means you must "get into the buyer's head," find out what the buyer *really* wants, and provide the means of satisfying that desire. Therefore, any interviews you go on must be focused on what the interviewer needs and what problems he needs to have solved.

WHAT ARE THE MAIN REASONS WHY PEOPLE BUY (OR SAY YES, OR MAKE A COMMITMENT)?

There are many reasons people "buy," but here are four major categories:

1. *Money:* People are always concerned with making a profit and/or avoiding a loss. Everyone wants to make or save money; that's why it's so important that you link your Arsenal of Accomplishments to dollars or percents. If you've been able to make or save money for an employer in the past, chances are you'll be able to do it again.
   - Can you show that you've been able to save money in the past, either for yourself or for someone else?
   - Can you show how you would apply that ability to a potential employer's needs?

2. *Recognition and acceptance by others:* Interviewers need to feel that hiring you, or passing you on to others who might hire you, will enhance their recognition and acceptance by others, because if you turn out to be a disappointment, it will reflect badly on them.

- Can you demonstrate that a decision to "buy your product" will be a reflection of their good judgment?

3. *Feeling good:* Everyone wants to feel good about themselves, to take pride in what they do, their reputation, and their position.

- Can you assure an interviewer that he or she is making a smart decision by recommending you or hiring you?
- Can you demonstrate that you can relieve some worry or solve some problem?

4. *Looking good:* Not only do we all want to look good, we all want to buy products that enhance our appearance and the way we feel about ourselves. Interviewers are drawn to people who take pride in themselves and their appearance.

- Do your looks and demeanor reflect the way you think about yourself and the way you'd like others to see you?

WHAT IS THE MOST IMPORTANT FIRST STEP IN AN INTERVIEW OR IN "MAKING A SALE"?

One of the most important aspects of selling yourself in an interview is to *build rapport* with the interviewer. One of the central principles of the sales trade is that *people buy from people they like, trust, and respect.*

People like you when you're on the same wavelength as they are—when they feel you're concerned about their needs as well as your own. That is why it is crucial to ask questions and find out what the employer really needs. If you can hone in on those needs, and let the employer know you're the one who can fill them, you'll have a much better chance at reaching your interview goal.

People trust you when you're forthright and honest—when you're up-front and confident about who you are and what your goals are. Since you have gone over your Arsenal of Accomplishments and you've discovered your hidden skills, you can talk about yourself with pride and assurance. You don't have to brag, and you certainly don't have to lie about what you have or haven't done. Your purpose is to let the interviewer know that you have the knowledge, skills, and experience to be of service.

People respect you when you treat them with respect. People sense a bad attitude a mile away. The Golden Rule applies to everyone—including interviewers.

SELLING YOURSELF IN ALL TYPES OF INTERVIEWS

ON WHAT TYPES OF INTERVIEWS WILL I USE MY SELLING SKILLS?

You may be tempted to save up all your selling skills to use when you finally get in to see "the boss." However, you must sell yourself in every interview situation in order to get the most out of your job-hunting adventure.

HOW CAN I USE NETWORKING AS A SALES OPPORTUNITY?

Suppose you go on a networking, or referral, interview

(in this case, "go on" could mean a formal visit to an executive's office or bumping into an old friend on the street). No matter how informal the encounter, you are still in an interview situation. You are selling yourself to this person so that he or she will recommend you to a more appropriate buyer.

PICTURE THIS:

You are walking down the street, daydreaming and window-shopping. You're just about to cross a busy intersection when someone taps you on the shoulder. You turn around and realize it is Fred Reilly. You and Fred worked together in the same office for almost two years, but you haven't seen him since you left that job about four years ago.

Fred immediately goes into a long sad story about how he was laid off six months ago and hasn't been able to find another job. He goes on and on about all the "bad" interviews he's had, and all the rejection he's suffered. He finishes by saying, "Hey, maybe you know someone who could give me a job!"

What would you do? You'd probably say "I'll think about it," and walk away knowing you'll never pass Fred's number on to anyone. *There's nothing in it for you.* Fred did nothing to sell himself to you; he only reinforced his inability to do well at interviews. You certainly wouldn't want to risk your good name and reputation by recommending a "loser" like Fred.

Fred may be very good at what he does. He may be an ideal employee in many ways, but until he learns to sell himself, he'll have a hard time finding a job.

Whenever you find yourself in a networking situation, let the "interviewer" know that you are reliable and dependable, that you are worthy of the time and effort she will take to connect you with someone. Make her feel that she will benefit by recommending you, that you will make her look good to her contacts.

HOW CAN I SELL MYSELF TO EMPLOYMENT AGENCIES AND HEADHUNTERS?

Just as the boss has a lot at stake when making hiring decisions, employment agencies, headhunters, and personnel managers have a lot at stake by sending you on to see the boss.

Most employment agencies make their money only when someone they recommend is hired. Although these agencies have a reputation for sending lots of people up for the same job (so that *somebody* they sent over will get hired and they can make their commission), they are looking for the *best* people to send to the best jobs. Their clients will complain and probably withdraw their business if the quality of prospective employees drops below a certain level. You want to be sure that you are considered for the best, and most appropriate, jobs.

Headhunters usually contact you first—but that doesn't mean they're entirely sold on you. They don't want to risk their reputations on someone who is not going to make them look good. They, too, are anxious to keep their clients' business.

Employment agencies and headhunters will be looking closely at your résumé, because the prospective employer has presented them with a list of *logical* requirements for the job: "I need someone with such and such skills, this many years' experience, etc." The agency will try to fill those requests as closely as possible.

But they are also asking themselves, "What's in it for me?" So you must keep your public-relations and selling skills honed when dealing with both employment agencies and headhunters. They want you to make them look good, so they are also interested in your most basic need-filling abilities. If you want to be sent up for a particular job, but you don't fill all the logical requirements, you must use your selling skills to show the interviewer how the abilities you do have will fulfill the boss's needs. Draw on your Arsenal of Accomplishments to demonstrate your abilities to be a team player, to be a decision maker and a problem solver.

HOW DO I SELL MYSELF TO PERSONNEL MANAGERS?

The same principles apply for personnel managers. Their job is to weed people out, and to select only those who match the requirements given them by the prospective boss. A personnel manager must "pass on" only those applicants she feels fit the boss's requirements perfectly—otherwise, her job may be on the line. If you deviate in any way from the boss's list, you'll have to rely on your selling skills to get the manager back on your side.

In order to find out what employment agencies, headhunters, and personnel managers really need, and what they're really looking for, you're going to have to ask questions. The types of questions you should be asking will be discussed in the individual chapters dealing with each of these interview situations.

BELIEVE IN THE VALUE OF YOUR PRODUCT

There is another very important principle of the sales trade.

SECRET STRATEGY NUMBER 7:
Believe in the value of your own product—
YOU—or no one else will believe enough to buy.

ISN'T SELLING MYSELF SELLING OUT?

Many people feel awkward or embarrassed about selling themselves—because they equate it with being pushy and conceited. A lot of us have been taught that it's not nice to talk about ourselves. But that's not what selling yourself is all about. You're not trying to brag, lie, or cheat your way into a job. That's an old-fashioned notion of selling. Nowadays, a successful salesperson is someone who asks questions and listens instead of bulldozing his or her way through a sale.

A successful salesperson sees him or herself as someone whose purpose is to help others solve problems. That's exactly what you're doing when you're looking for a job. You're trying to match up your talents and abilities with an employer who has a problem you can solve or a need you can fill.

Selling yourself *does not* mean selling out. You're only selling out if you don't make every possible effort to follow your dreams and to get what you want. You are selling out if you don't believe in yourself enough to sell it to somebody else.

Enthusiasm is catching. If you have a positive attitude about yourself and your ability to do the job, the interviewer will feel it, too.

You can't expect every interview you go on to be an unqualified success. But you can expect that you will give 100 percent to every interview you go on. Every time you set out to "make a sale," remind yourself that you are a unique, special individual with a lot of talent and a genuine contribution to make.

SPECIAL CON-SIDERATIONS: THE HIGHER-LEVEL EXECUTIVE AND PROFESSIONAL

It's tough for anyone to be out of work. Whatever your circumstances, there are challenges you'll have to face. If you are an executive or professional, perhaps facing unemployment for the first time in your career, there are particular problems to be solved.

These problems are not insurmountable. In fact, you probably have many advantages over people who are just starting out, or who have not yet attained your professional level.

CONSIDER YOUR ADVANTAGES

WHAT ARE THE ADVANTAGES I HAVE GAINED?

Some of those advantages are:

1. *Contacts:* If you've been working in your field long enough to attain a managerial position, then you must have made contacts along the way. This includes *everyone* you've associated with over the years: former employers, former staff, colleagues from other divisions within your company, vendors and suppliers, "rival" employers, association members, etc. All of these people are good sources for networking and/or information interviews.

2. *Associations:* Most people in higher-level positions already belong to some kind of trade or professional association. Do not let your membership lapse just because you're presently unemployed. Many associations have job-placement services, or newsletters in which open positions are advertised. And, of course, association meetings are perfect venues for honing your networking skills.

3. *References and referrals:* In times past, a high-level executive was usually out of work due to poor performance on the job. Nowadays, your performance level may have nothing to do with the reason you're unemployed. Companies are closing and downsizing all over the United States, and many of the country's best and brightest are finding themselves in unfortunate circumstances. The positive side of this is that employers who are forced to let people go due to the state of the economy are usually more than happy to supply references and give referrals whenever possible. Don't be shy about asking; there's nothing like a glowing recommendation to give you a competitive edge.

4. *Salable skills:* People with little or no experience may have a tough time uncovering skills that are uni-

versally applicable, but managerial skills are always in demand. The more experience you have, the more skills you have to sell. It's easier to learn the ins and outs of a new company or industry than it is to learn how to be a good manager. This knowledge and experience are often of great importance to companies undergoing change, and can be one of your greatest selling points.

5. *Severance pay:* This won't be true for everyone, of course. But many companies are offering high-level executives early retirement packages or attractive severance deals so that they can downsize without having to lay off so many people. If you are able to take advantage of such a situation, you can start your job search with a small financial cushion. Many lower-level employees are simply let go without warning, and are given little or no compensation.

FACTOR IN THE DISADVANTAGES

ARE THERE DISADVANTAGES AS WELL?

I'm not trying to paint an overly bright picture of executives' prospects. There are disadvantages for this group as well:

1. *Fewer available jobs:* Since many companies are closing and downsizing, the number of managerial positions available has greatly decreased. People who have not been let go are staying firmly put, afraid to give up their security. So the competition for any one job can be very intense.

2. *Age:* An experienced executive is likely to be middle-aged or older, and although it is illegal to discrimi-

nate on the basis of age, the reality is that it happens all the time. Some employers feel they will get innovation or energy from a younger employee that they won't get from an older one. And, of course, a younger, less experienced employee will probably work for less money than an older, more experienced executive.

3. *Lack of flexibility:* If you have been in one job, or worked within one particular industry for many years, change can be difficult. Your area of expertise may have become outdated, or your industry may have been hit harder than most, making it almost impossible to get a position even remotely similar to one you've held in the past. The feeling of having to "start all over" can be overwhelming.

4. *Standard of living:* Everything is relative. Although as an executive you may receive a generous severance package, you may also have more responsibilities and higher upkeep than someone just starting out. You may have a larger home, and have children in college to support. You may be the sole support of your family. You and your family may have to make numerous life-style adjustments until you find new employment.

5. *Ego:* This is a problem that is not often discussed in job-search or interviewing books. But ego can be a great disadvantage to an executive or professional —unless it is dealt with properly. It can be a great blow to your pride to be laid off after a long and distinguished career. It's important to remember that most people are being let go for economic reasons, not personal ones.

   Another ego factor is that executives are simply used to having things done for them. A close friend of mine, an executive vice-president of a financial corporation, was let go after seventeen years with the company. He talked to me about some of the difficulties he was having looking for a new job. "I've spent most of my career making major decisions," he said. "I'm not used to doing the detail work myself." He was having a hard time adjusting to his new circumstances—writing his own letters, going to the copy center to get his résumé duplicated, even learning the computer, which he had never had to use before. He was used to having an entire support system behind him, and now he felt lost without it.

TAKE APPROPRIATE ACTION

WHAT'S THE BEST WAY TO OVERCOME THE DISADVANTAGES?

The disadvantages listed above may be obstacles, but they are not barriers. Many executives have seen their layoffs as perfect opportunities to pursue long-held dreams of a different occupation, a life-style change, or a chance to start a business of their own. You can use your advantages to outweigh any problems you may have.

WHERE DO I START?

First, use your contacts. Sharpen your networking skills (see Section 10) and get in touch with everyone you know. Don't be embarrassed to say you're out of work—millions of others are in the same boat. Stay in touch with your contacts. The longer you're out of work, the more important it is to keep your name fresh in your contacts' minds. Jot them a line every few weeks with holiday or birthday greetings, or send them newspaper or magazine articles they may find interesting.

HOW CAN I BEST TAKE ADVANTAGE OF MY ASSOCIATION MEMBERSHIPS?

Read the information on associations in the next section. Keep up, and keep *active* in your association. You want to get yourself known to people in your industry. Run for office, or volunteer to join (or head) a committee. Go to association events or conferences. These endeavors may cost you money, but consider it an investment in your future.

I'VE BEEN OFFERED SOME PART-TIME WORK AT A NEARBY FIRM. SHOULD I TAKE IT, OR SHOULD I HOLD OUT FOR A FULL-TIME POSITION?

Accept part-time or temporary work whenever possible. A good approach may be to offer your services as a consultant or as a trainer (you might even want to discuss this option with your employer as soon as you find out you are being laid off). A company that may not be able to afford a full-time experienced manager may need someone to oversee a short-term project. Or, they may have cut back their staff to the point where the people still there are inexperienced and insecure. They might just be hungry for someone who can come in on a temporary basis and train their staff. These types of free-lance or consulting assignments are often the best way to make valuable contacts (while getting paid) and find full-time employment.

If a company you're approaching for either full-time or

free-lance work is not familiar with your work, and you really want the job, offer to bring in a sample or to work a few days or a week with no pay. Never refer to your need for the job, however. Instead, offer to help the company out of a tough situation. You might say, "I know how difficult it is to hire someone you don't know at all. If you have any doubts about me, let me do a sample design for you on spec." Or, "Bring me in for a week, gratis. Then you'll be able to see how effectively I can get this project off the ground."

INTERVIEWING FROM THE OTHER SIDE

I HAVE NOT BEEN AN "INTERVIEWEE" FOR QUITE SOME TIME. IS THIS A PROBLEM?

To the contrary. Most executives have an advantage because they've conducted interviews themselves. If you've been on the hiring side of the desk, then you know what you looked for during an interview. You may want to write down some of your most successful interviewing techniques, and how the best candidates handled your approach. It won't take long for you to "think like a boss," since you have that experience behind you.

WHAT IF THE INTERVIEWS I CONDUCTED WERE NOT SO SUCCESSFUL?

If you have not conducted successful interviews, and didn't hire good people, use the same writing exercise to analyze what you missed. Every job seeker needs to practice, no matter how long or short a time it's been between interviews. Practicing the questioning, listening, and interviewing skills in the chapters ahead can easily take care of any nervousness or stress you may feel at facing an interviewer.

"SORRY, YOU'RE OVERQUALIFIED. . . ."

I HAVE BEEN ON SEVERAL INTERVIEWS WHERE I'VE BEEN TOLD THAT I'M OVERQUALIFIED. WHAT CAN I DO ABOUT THIS?

Job opportunities at the level you were at when you were laid off may not be readily available. As an executive, you are then faced with applying for jobs at a lower level—and a lower salary—than you had before.

Many employers will look at your résumé and say, "You were a vice-president for ten years, you were making $75,000. This job does not have the same level of responsibility, and only pays $50,000. You're overqualified." What can you do to combat this stereotypical response? You have to use a special technique in interviewing—you have to sell yourself by *underselling* yourself.

HOW DO I UNDERSELL MYSELF?

Don't go into an interview and talk about how much money you've made in the past. Instead of emphasizing what you've accomplished, emphasize how your skills would fit into the present situation, and how you've always been a team player. Concentrate on the employer's needs, and how you can fill them.

MANY INTERVIEWERS SEEM TO FEEL THAT BECAUSE I WAS PREVIOUSLY MAKING A HIGH SALARY, I WON'T STAY IN A POSITION THAT PAYS LESS. HOW CAN I CONVINCE THEM OTHERWISE?

The interviewer has probably stated to many candidates, "This job does not have the prestige or the salary of your previous employment. Do you think you could be happy here?" If your answer to him is yes, but your answer deep inside yourself is no, don't take this job. If you can truthfully say that you'll be able—and willing—to make any necessary adjustments, ease the employer's concerns by focusing on what you can do for him if you take this position.

Try the direct approach. You might say, "You're probably interviewing less experienced people because they're willing to work for less money. But I know, because of my background, I can do the job and save your company money." Then bring up something from your Arsenal of Accomplishments that shows how you saved, or made, your company money in the past. Then tell the potential boss, "I know I can do the same for you. I'd be willing to start at a lower salary, if in six months you evaluate my performance. If you find that I am indeed saving you money, then raise my salary." Not everyone will agree to this suggestion. But a smart employer will.

ON MY LAST JOB, I WAS EARNING $75,000. NOW I'M INTERVIEWING FOR JOBS THAT PAY $50,000 OR EVEN LESS. HOW DO I ACCEPT AN OFFER OF LESS MONEY WITHOUT UNDERCUTTING MY VALUE?

First, you must decide if this is a job in which you can be happy. Even if you've been out of work for a long period, taking a job you hate is not the answer. You will not be helping yourself or your family if you spend your life in misery.

Second, learn not to equate your value with your salary.

SECRET STRATEGY NUMBER 8
Your value lies in your skills and experience,
and your attitude toward your own self-worth—
not in how much money you make.

Times are tough, and even an excellent book on interviewing can't cure all the economic ills of the world. However, every step you take toward improving your skills improves your chances of getting the kinds of job offers you want and deserve.

In the past few chapters you've learned how to gather information about yourself and about the companies and employers for whom you'd like to work. You've learned what interviewers are really looking for, and the fundamentals of selling yourself. The next step is to go out and get those interviews! There are many ways to accomplish this goal, and the next chapter will explore each of them.

SECTION 6

SMART QUESTIONS TO ASK ABOUT GETTING AN INTERVIEW: SECRET STRATEGIES FOR BEATING THE INTER- VIEW ODDS

What is the most important, and often most difficult, aspect of the interviewing pro- cess? *Getting* the inter- view. Bosses are busy. If they're not actively hiring, they may feel they're too busy to grant any kind of interview, or that they have to be very selective about who they see. If they are actively advertising to fill a position, they may be inundated with phone calls or letters and résumés.

It is possible to beat the odds, however, by using as many interview resources as there are available to you. If the only thing you do is answer want ads from the Sunday paper, or register with one employment agency, you're severely limiting your possibilities. Study all the resources listed in this section (and any other resources you may think of). Some will garner better results than others, but all of them are worth a try. You want to find sources for information interviews and networking interviews as well as standard job interviews. Your goal is to get as many interviews as you possibly can.

CLASSIFIED ADS

WHAT ARE THE ADVANTAGES OF USING CLASSIFIED ADS AS A SOURCE FOR INTERVIEWS?

The advantage of want ads (also known as classified ads) is that you can scan the paper quickly and come up with several leads in a short period of time.

WHAT ARE THE DISADVANTAGES OF USING CLASSIFIED ADS AS A SOURCE FOR INTERVIEWS?

What's the first thing that most people do when they're looking for a job? They buy the paper and look through the want ads. In large cities especially, the competition can be fierce. Don't ignore this potential job source, but realize that only about 10 percent of all jobs filled come from answering classified ads.

WHEN DO EMPLOYERS USUALLY PLACE CLASSIFIED ADS?

Employers often use want ads only after they've tried everything else. First, they look for employees within their own company who may be able to fill the position. Then they rely on word of mouth, networking, and referrals. If none of these options pans out, they may put an ad in the paper.

TO WHOM ARE CLASSIFIED ADS USUALLY GEARED?

Classified ads are usually geared toward entry-to-middle-level jobs. It's also difficult to get interviews through the want ads if you're looking to change careers and will need a lot of training. In his book *How to Get Interviews from Job Ads*, Kenneth W. Elderkin states, "Job advertisements are oriented toward your past. They are not oriented toward your potential."

I SAW AN AD IN THE PAPER THAT INTERESTS ME. HOWEVER, I DON'T FIT ALL THE QUALIFICATIONS LISTED. SHOULD I ANSWER IT ANYWAY?

When employers do place ads, they often list the qualifications of an ideal employee. For instance, an ad may read:

> *Executive assistant needed, extremely busy office. College grad., 5 yrs. experience, 85 wpm, knowledge of Word Perfect 5.1.*

Many people will look at that ad and, if they don't meet every one of those qualifications, pass it by—which is what the employer had in mind. She may not expect you to match the qualifications 100 percent, but she wants to weed out those people who don't even come close.

When you are scanning the classifieds, look for ads that list qualifications similar or related to qualifications you already possess. Ask yourself:

- Which qualifications do I have that match up exactly?
- Which qualifications do I have that can be easily transferred to the ones listed, or that I can learn quickly and easily?

•Which qualifications do I not have at all?

Suppose you read the ad listed above. You did not go to college, but you have three years of experience working for a top-level executive in a high-pressure environment. You type about 75 wpm, and know a different word-processing system. Should you apply for the job? Certainly! Don't ask yourself: Can I do this job perfectly this minute? Ask yourself: Can I learn to do this job with a little time and a little training? If you can truthfully answer yes to this question, answer the ad.

WHAT IS THE BEST WAY TO RESPOND TO A CLASSIFIED AD?

Remember that the initial purpose of answering an ad is not to get you a job offer, but to *get you an interview.* If at all possible, you want to get to the employer separately from all the other people answering the ad. The ad may request that you send your résumé to the company; it may even give you the name of a person to whom you should address your letter. Don't assume, however, that the person listed is the person in charge of filling the position. The person listed could be someone in personnel, or a secretary whose job it is to read through the replies and weed out "unqualified" candidates.

Call the company directly. Don't refer to the ad. Ask who is the division president or the head of the department to which you're applying. If it's a small company, ask for the name of the president. Be sure you get the correct spelling and proper title.

Write a sales-oriented letter. Using your Arsenal of Accomplishments as a foundation, include one or two of your outstanding achievements, and how they relate to your ability to help the person and the company to whom you are writing (see section 9 for more details on writing cover letters). Once again, don't mention the ad. Make it appear as if it's just a coincidence that you're writing to the boss at the very time she's looking to hire someone.

SECRET STRATEGY NUMBER 9:
When answering a classified ad, don't apologize for,
or even mention, the fact that you lack
some of the qualifications listed in the ad.

WHAT IF THE AD STATES TO CALL THE COMPANY INSTEAD OF SENDING A LETTER OR RÉSUMÉ?

Sometimes an ad lists a number to call. In that case, the company is probably in a hurry to hire someone. Try to call early in the day, if possible. There may be a limited number of interview slots available. You don't want to miss out on a good opportunity simply because you called too late.

If you do call, you will usually be interviewed, or at least screened, over the phone. Be prepared. Write down your qualifications beforehand. Have your list of accomplishments handy. Speak clearly and distinctly. Be friendly; use the person's name during the conversation. Don't tell everything there is to tell about yourself. This is usually a preliminary interview; you'll still have to come in for a face-to-face.

IF I GET SOMEONE ON THE PHONE, SHOULD I USE THAT OPPORTUNITY TO GET INFORMATION ABOUT THE COMPANY?

If you are speaking to a secretary or receptionist, this

could be a good opportunity for you to get information. If possible, ask:

- What is the name and title of the person who will be doing the hiring?
- Can you tell me anything about him/her?
- What are the details of the position to be filled?
- What can you tell me about the company? Is there any written information that can be mailed out?
- When can I make an appointment for an in-person interview?

NEWSPAPERS, MAGAZINES, AND TRADE PUBLICATIONS

SECRET STRATEGY NUMBER 10:
Read the *entire* paper or magazine, not just the want ads, to get interview leads.

WHAT OTHER PARTS OF THE PAPER, BESIDES THE WANT ADS, ARE USEFUL FOR FINDING INTERVIEW LEADS?

- Read the business section of your newspaper, as well as business-oriented magazines.
- Read feature articles about new businesses opening up and older businesses expanding.
- Check out the announcements of promotions; newly promoted managers often prefer to bring in outsiders so that they can build up their own team.
- Look over the listings of new appointments and notice where a newly appointed executive held his or her last job. That company may be looking for a replacement.

- Read profiles of successful executives, and use these feature stories as leads for information and networking interviews.

WHAT SHOULD I DO IF I FIND AN ARTICLE OR PROFILE THAT SEEMS LIKE A POSSIBLE LEAD?

As we will discuss in detail in the section on information interviews, send the executive a letter that does not imply that you are asking this person for a job. Congratulate her on her promotion or new appointment, and ask if she might be able to spare you a half hour to talk about the industry. Give her a taste of your background, and why you want this data, but remember the object here is to get information, not a job offer (although you should always remain open to the possibility that this type of interview may lead to a job offer).

WHAT ABOUT PROFESSIONAL PUBLICATIONS AND TRADE JOURNALS?

These are also good sources of interview possibilities. These types of publications (which can usually be found in the periodicals section of the library) are often geared toward specific industries, and have very good classified sections. Keep the odds in mind here, too. There will probably be a large number of people with similar qualifications applying for these positions. That doesn't mean you shouldn't go for it; just don't be surprised if you get a rejection or no response at all. To beat the odds, use the same techniques you'd use for other classified ads—try to get directly to the person who is doing the hiring.

PROFESSIONAL ASSOCIATIONS AND ALUMNI ORGANIZATIONS

HOW CAN I USE PROFESSIONAL ASSOCIATIONS FOR GETTING INTERVIEW LEADS?

You know the old saying, "It's not what you know, it's who you know that counts"? Well, you can get to "know" hundreds, even thousands of people by joining organizations that may provide interview possibilities.

Just about every industry today has a professional association attached to it. Many of these associations offer job-placement assistance for their members. They may publish the type of magazine or journal discussed above. They may offer a "job phone" or "job bank," which allows you to call (sometimes for an additional fee) and get interview leads. Associations may also sponsor job fairs where you can interview with several potential employers in one day.

Associations also offer excellent opportunities for getting information and for networking. They often have local, regional, and national meetings where you can mix and mingle with others in your field. If you're new to the industry, you can strike up a conversation and conduct an informal information interview. If you have more experience in the field, these meetings are perfect occasions for networking.

HOW DO I KNOW WHAT ASSOCIATIONS EXIST FOR THE INDUSTRY IN WHICH I'M INTERESTED?

If you don't know what's available to you, go to the library and check the *Encyclopedia of Associations* to find out which ones would be of interest to you.

HOW CAN I USE MY ALUMNI ORGANIZATION FOR GETTING INTERVIEW LEADS?

Many universities have job-placement offices whose services are available to older alumni as well as current graduates. However, these organizations often have little more than a bulletin board or job listing service. You'll usually be given a name and address (and possibly a phone number) and a few vague facts about the available position.

It is up to you to turn this into an interview advantage. Do your research. Find out about the company. If possible, find out more about the job. Ask the alumni office if the person who placed the ad is also an alumni (this is often the case). If this is true, be sure to mention your mutual background in your cover letter or initial phone conversation.

JOB FAIRS

WHAT IS A JOB FAIR?

These are usually one- or two-day affairs where a large group of employers set up booths or tables and provide interview opportunities for job-fair attendees. These fairs are usually sponsored by universities, alumni organizations, professional and trade associations, and corporate groups.

ARE JOB FAIRS A GOOD SOURCE OF INTERVIEW LEADS?

Usually held at a local hotel or conference center, job fairs at least give you a chance to talk to an actual human being. These fairs are often geared to entry-level jobs (although some include opportunities for mid-to-higher-level jobs), so they are not for everyone. They can be a good source for information interviews, however, and may give you a feel for the kinds of people you're likely to encounter in a particular industry.

WHAT DO I NEED TO KNOW ABOUT THE FAIR BEFORE I GET THERE?

If you're planning to attend a job fair, it pays to find out the details before you go. Call up the group sponsoring the fair and ask:

- What is the admission fee for the fair?
- Are there any other fees involved—for instance, if you are hired by one of the participating companies, will you have to pay any fees either to the company or the group sponsoring the fair?
- What types of positions are attending employers offering?
- How many companies will be represented?
- How many attendees do they expect?
- What is the procedure for obtaining interviews with the participating companies? Do you just stand in line? Do you sign up in advance?
- How long does an average interview last?
- What do you need to bring with you? Your résumé? Your portfolio?

WHAT IS THE ADVANTAGE OF ATTENDING A JOB FAIR?

The main advantage of attending a job fair is that you can usually talk to several employers in one day without having to spend extra travel time or money.

WHAT IS THE DISADVANTAGE OF ATTENDING A JOB FAIR?

The disadvantage of attending a job fair is that the employer is also talking to several people on that day. Because all the people attending are there with the same purpose is mind, it is very difficult to stand out from the crowd. You don't want to do anything outrageous (because that will probably keep you from being hired), but you do want to be remembered.

WHAT CAN I DO TO STAND OUT AND BE REMEMBERED?

You might try something simple like carrying business cards, or having pencils made up with your name on them. Then when you speak to someone about an interview possibility, you can hand them a card or a pencil and let them know you'll be contacting them again shortly. Or you may want to wear something special to which you can refer, such as a brightly colored tie, suspenders, or an unusual pin (I always wear pins in the shape of question marks, of course).

I WENT TO A JOB FAIR AND SPOKE TO A REPRESENTATIVE OF A COMPANY I'D LIKE TO WORK FOR. THE REPRESENTATIVE ALSO SEEMED INTERESTED IN ME. WHAT SHOULD I DO NEXT?

Interviews at the job fair are usually brief because there are many people to see. But ask as many questions as the time will allow. Find out if the person with whom you are speaking is the person who will do the hiring (this is usually *not* the case). Jot down the names of both the person you've spoken to and the potential boss. Write to both of them.

In your letter to the interviewer, remind him of where you met. Mention that you were the one with the stenciled pencil, or the pin in the shape of a fox terrier—anything to jog his memory so that he can remember who you are. Perhaps recall a bit of conversation you had: "I enjoyed our conversation about the possibility of the company headquarters moving to Dallas." Thank him for the time he spent with you; then add that you will call next week to schedule a more in-depth interview.

Also write to the potential supervisor directly. If the interviewer won't give you the boss's name at the job fair, use the same techniques as above. Call the company and ask for the head of the division or the president of the company. If your interview at the job fair went well, mention this in the letter. If it didn't, don't even mention that you attended the fair. Do, however, mention any interesting facts or related information you discovered at the fair that make you think you'd like to work at this company.

Every interview you go on is practice for the next one. The more you go on the better you'll be. Now you know that you need to think like a boss, and you need to be able to sell yourself from his perspective in order to satisfy his emotional needs. But how can you be sure exactly what it is he needs? The only way to find out where people are coming from is through a planned process of asking questions and active listening. The next chapter will tell you how to hone and perfect those two important skills.

SECTION 7

SMART QUESTIONS TO ASK ABOUT TECHNIQUE: HOW TO HONE QUESTIONING & LISTENING SKILLS

Do you know how to ask a question to get the information you need? Do you know how to listen—with your eyes as well as your ears? Most of us think we do. The problem is that we don't always ask the right questions, and we don't always listen to hear what we need to know.

There are two major ways of getting information. One, the more passive way, is by watching and reading. The second, and interactive way, is by asking and listening. Since you're always better off taking an active role in an interview, you need to practice and perfect your questioning and listening skills.

*   *   *

THE POWER OF QUESTIONS

SHOULDN'T I BE DOING ALL THE TALKING AT AN INTERVIEW?

It's tempting to think of an interview as an opportunity to tell someone just how wonderful you really are. After all, the interviewer is asking you questions, and you want to answer completely. You hate to leave anything out. You think the more you tell about yourself and your outstanding accomplishments, the more you'll be able to convince the employment agency to send you out on interviews, to persuade personnel to pass you on to the next level, or to induce the boss to hire you. Not so.

When you're in an interview situation, you are, in effect, a salesperson, selling the product (you) to a potential buyer. The best salespeople are those who help the buyer discover the connection between his needs and the product the salesperson is offering. A good salesperson finds out why a buyer wants a particular product or service. For example, someone buying an air conditioner obviously wants to keep cool. But if she's looking for a particular type, style, or size of air conditioner, the salesperson must find out why. Perhaps the buyer has a small apartment with narrow windows, and is therefore limited as to the size and strength of the air conditioner she can purchase. Once the salesperson has this information, he can direct the buyer toward those models that will suit her needs.

HOW DO I SELL MYSELF AT AN INTERVIEW?

The interviewer is looking for a person to fill an open position. It is your job to find out exactly what the employer needs to fill that position satisfactorily, and then to let him know that you can fill those needs. The only way you can make that connection is to show the employer how his needs connect with your talents, abilities, and personal characteristics.

WHY IS ASKING QUESTIONS SO IMPORTANT?

If you are doing all the talking, you have no way of finding out the information you need to know. And the only way that you are going to get the other person talking is by asking a question. A question is a very powerful communications tool. In fact, there are five great powers of questions:

1. *Questions give you information.* This is the most obvious power of questions, yet it's one that is often overlooked (and underused) in interview situations. Even in information interviews, when the point is to gather as much information as possible, most people end up talking the whole time, or if they do ask questions, they don't get the answers they really need.

   You've got to know the purpose of every interview you go on, exactly what type of information you're looking for, and the kinds of questions you need to ask to get you that information. For instance, if you're going to an initial interview at an employment agency, you may not be able to ask for specific information about a company or a particular employer—because the agency doesn't yet know where it will send you. However, you could ask questions like:

   - What kinds of companies do you generally have as clients?
   - How do you go about matching up jobs and applicants?

•How much do you know about the jobs and/or the employers before you send applicants out for the position?

If you're in a one-on-one interview situation with a potential boss, you must also use questions to get information. You have two objectives when you go in for this type of interview:
1. To get a job offer
2. To get information about the job and the company

Your ultimate goal is always to get a job offer—you can always turn it down. However, your second, and equally important objective is to find out as much information as you possibly can about the job, the company, and your potential boss. You need this information so that you can make a sound decision as to whether or not you want the job—and whether to accept the job or not should always be *your* decision.

SECRET STRATEGY NUMBER 11:
You're not just going to be interviewed—you're going to interview your interviewer!

2. *Questions demand answers.* The main reason that questions are so effective is that most people love to answer them. One of the axioms of human communications is that most people prefer talking to listening. Although the interviewer may intend to do all the listening while you do all the talking, she'll be secretly pleased to talk when you ask her questions.
3. *Questions put you in control.* What would you do with the rest of your life if you just won a million dollars? Got you thinking about it, didn't I? Just by asking one simple question, I changed the direction

of your thoughts. By asking the right questions in an interview situation, you can steer the conversation in the direction you want it to go. The smarter the questions you ask, the more control you have. Each time you answer an interviewer's question, regain control of the situation by asking a question of your own (we'll discuss the kinds of questions you should be asking in later sections).

4. *Questions stimulate thought.* Think about what it is you really want to know. Posing a question takes more concentration than making a statement; it also forces the other person to think more clearly before answering. To answer you, he must organize his own thoughts and put them into words.

   Suppose you're in a networking interview—an informal one with a friend of the family. If you ask, "Do you know anyone who can hire me?" you're forcing this person to go through a list of everyone she knows and answer you immediately. Chances are she'll simply say "No, I don't." Ask instead, "Do you know anyone who's been complaining about their computer system lately? I'm an experienced computer programmer, and I could probably help them out." That way, not only do you get your friend thinking specifically, you get her to realize that she will be helping someone out by recommending that her contact speak with you.

   In a one-on-one situation, you want to find out the real scoop about a job before you decide whether or not to take it. You don't just want to hear an employer's pat, rehearsed job description—the same one he tells every candidate.

5. *Questions show that you care.* Have you ever been on a blind date? Or struck up a conversation with someone at a party? What is your impression if that

person talks on and on about himself, his work and his hobbies, and doesn't ask any questions about you and what you do? You probably think that person is a terrible bore, and you definitely think that person doesn't care anything about you.

The same thing is true of interviews. If you talk incessantly about yourself, your past experience, and your hopes for the future, you may not come off as boring—but you'll certainly give the impression that you don't care. Suppose you're in an interview with a personnel manager (even though it's best to avoid personnel interviews, it's not always possible). If you sit there like a bump on a log and don't show some initiative, some curiosity, and some concern by asking questions of your own, the manager is not likely to consider passing your résumé on to the person who might actually hire you—no matter how qualified you are for the job.

DON'T I ALREADY ASK ENOUGH QUESTIONS?

Most of us think we ask enough questions. But how many times have you gone to an interview, and when the interviewer asked, "Do you have any questions?" you simply answered no. What kind of impression do you think that makes? As a boss, I know. It makes me think the person hasn't been listening, doesn't really want the job, and/or doesn't care enough about me or my company.

A manager I know once told me, "I wouldn't hire a person who didn't ask me some questions during the interview. If the candidate doesn't ask me anything about the job, I figure he's a self-centered, passive sort of person. If he does ask me at least a few questions, it tells me that he's interested."

THE TWO TYPES OF QUESTIONS

There are many different types of questions, but most fall into two broad categories: the *closed* question, one that extracts a piece of information but precludes further discussion, and the *open* question, one that stimulates thought and encourages continued conversation.

WHAT IS A CLOSED QUESTION?

A closed question can be answered with a yes or no, or with a simple statement of fact. They are good for getting direct information. Here are some examples:

- How many people work in this department?
- Who is responsible for quality control?
- Does this agency charge a fee?
- Do you know someone who might hire me?

WHAT IS AN OPEN QUESTION?

An open question requires a more in-depth response than a yes or no or a simple statement of fact. It creates a conversational tone, and encourages the other person to think about her answer. For instance, on an information interview, you ask the closed question, "Does your job require computer skills?" The person you're asking might just answer, "Yes, it does." That doesn't help you very much. But if you phrase it as an open question, "Can you tell me about some of the computer skills you need in a job like this?" the other person will probably give you a lot of useful information.

Some other examples of open questions are:

- What are the responsibilities of this job?
- Why is this position open?
- What would you most like for a new employee to bring to this job?

WHY ARE OPEN QUESTIONS SO USEFUL?

With open questions you gain more than factual information—you get a good take on thoughts, attitudes, and emotions that influence the other person's actions. Open questions often enable you to clue into an interviewer's personal opinion about a job or a potential employer, get more than just surface information from a variety of sources, and tune into a potential employer's emotional needs.

CLARIFYING THE SITUATION

The art of asking smart questions doesn't end with learning how to use open and closed questions. It's not enough to ask a question, get an answer, and let it go at that. You must be sure that you *understand* what the answer means.

WHY ARE CLARIFYING QUESTIONS SO IMPORTANT?

If you don't understand exactly what is being asked of you, you may answer in a way that harms your chances of being hired. Susan, a young friend of mine who is a single parent, called me up one day, disheartened and discouraged.

"I had a great interview today for a job I really want," she said, "but I don't think I'll get it."

"Why not?" I asked.

"Because," she said, "the boss asked if I would be willing to work overtime. I had to say no. I think I could have done this job really well, but I have to pick up my son from day-care every day at 5:30."

"How often would you have to work overtime?" I asked.

"I don't know," Susan replied. "He didn't say."

Luckily, Susan was called back for a second interview. This time, instead of saying no immediately when asked about overtime she said, "I'm not sure. How much overtime would be required?"

The boss answered, "Oh, not much. Once or twice a month, for only a few hours."

Susan knew that she could make arrangements for her mother to pick Billy up from school once or twice a month, and was able to answer yes to the overtime question. She got the job.

SECRET STRATEGY NUMBER 12:
Never answer an interviewer's question unless you're 100 percent certain you know what it means.

LEARN TO BE AN ACTIVE LISTENER

No matter how skilled you become at asking questions, it will do you no good unless you also learn how to listen. After all, a question is useless if you don't listen carefully to the response.

SOMETIMES I GET SO NERVOUS AT AN INTERVIEW, I FEEL LIKE I HAVEN'T HEARD ANYTHING THAT WAS SAID TO ME. HOW CAN I AVOID THAT SITUATION?

It's difficult to listen carefully when you're nervous. Most of us are nervous in interview situations—so practicing active listening skills is an important part of successful interviewing. Practice your skills in your everyday conversations. Try listening without interrupting. Repeat some of the main points your conversation partner has made.

One way to practice is to go on as many interviews as you possibly can—especially information interviews, where you don't have so much at stake. Knowing how to listen well will allow you to receive information as it's intended to be communicated. Epictetus, the Greek philosopher, once said, "God has wisely given us two ears and one mouth so we may hear twice as much as we speak."

HOW CAN I IMPROVE MY LISTENING SKILLS?

Listening well is a skill that requires concentration and effort. For one thing, it has been proven that we think at least four times faster than we can speak. So while we're listening, our minds are racing ahead. Thus we often project our own ideas, associations, and judgments onto what's being said to us. As a result, we're not fully tuned into what the other person is saying.

ISN'T LISTENING A PASSIVE SKILL? ISN'T IT SOMETHING WE JUST DO NATURALLY?

Most of us think of listening as a passive skill. After all, we've been listening to people all our lives. If you want to get the most out of every interview situation, however, you must learn to be an active listener. You must take responsibility for trying to grasp both the facts and the feelings behind what you hear. You must listen for both *content* and *intent*.

HOW DO I LISTEN FOR INTENT?

People don't always say what they really mean. Or they may not know what they mean themselves. Usually, however, people give you clues as to what they intend through the particular words they choose, through their tone of voice, or through their body language.

PICTURE THIS:
You're sitting in the boss's office, being interviewed for a position as her executive assistant. She is asking you whether or not you are familiar with a particular computer program used company-wide. You start to answer when you are interrupted by a phone call. It's a vendor, trying to sell the boss a new copy machine. After a brief conversation the boss hangs up, apologizes for the interruption, and says, "I shouldn't be getting these sales calls anyway. They should go directly to my vice-president. Now, you were telling me about your computer experience?"

You have just been given a major clue! Would you pick up on it? The clue is that this employer needs someone to screen her calls. If you go on a long explanation of all the computer experience you've ever had, and forget about the "incidental" interruption, you'll be missing out on a golden opportunity.

A better option might be to answer the boss's computer question quickly and completely, and end up by saying, "I did very well at keeping the bugs out of our system. I also did other types of 'bodyguard' duty. My former boss was very busy and hated unnecessary interruptions. So I became very good at screening phone calls and directing them to more appropriate personnel whenever possible."

It's a good bet that you will be high on this employer's list of possible candidates, because you tuned into her emotional need for someone to care enough to relieve her of annoying interruptions.

HOW DO I LEARN TO LISTEN ACTIVELY?

There are four steps to active listening:

1. *Concentrate*. When someone begins to talk, concentrate on what that person is saying. Don't think, "What am I going to say next?" Don't be so concerned with yourself that you forget to be concerned with what the other person is saying. If you're really listening, you'll know what to say when your turn comes.

2. *Summarize*. Mentally review what the other person is saying. Be sure you understand what is being said. If you're not sure, you may want to repeat the speaker's words and ask for clarification. For example, you might say, "You said earlier that to succeed in this business you've got to be ambitious and aggressive. Could you tell me how you define those terms?"

3. *Evaluate*. It's the ability to hear exactly what's being said, and to probe and clarify until the underlying meaning is crystal clear that sets apart the really skilled listener. These listeners notice even a subtle change in an interviewer's emotional temperature. Are you that observant? Imagine that a potential employer who was gung ho during your conversation ten minutes ago suddenly starts answering your questions abruptly and begins to wrap things up.

That drop in enthusiasm should be a warning to you. You might want to say, "A few minutes ago you seemed so excited. Are there some questions I haven't answered satisfactorily, or have I said something that concerns you?"

4. *Listen between the lines.* You've heard of reading between the lines? Listening between the lines means hearing not only words, but tone of voice and intonation as well. It also means "listening" with your eyes—be aware of facial expressions and body language. They often reveal more than words.

My mother always used to say, "I can't hear you, I don't have my glasses on." I used to think that was a really funny thing to say, but I have since come to realize that she knew what she was talking about.

We listen with all our senses, but especially with our eyes. If the interviewer is leaning forward, head slightly bent in your direction, it's usually a sign that he's interested in what you have to say. If, however, he's looking out the window and straightening out paper clips, you can be pretty sure he's not paying close attention. Then you may want to ask the same type of question you asked in step number 3.

It's very frustrating to know that you are the right person for the job, only to have the interview marred by an unnecessary lack of questioning and listening skills. These positive and powerful abilities will help you appear confident, caring, and in control—three very important elements in selling yourself to any interviewer.

In the next sections we'll talk about the various types of interviews you may run into, and how to use everything you've learned so far to be outstanding at each and every one of them.

PART II

THE PRE-EMPLOYER INTERVIEWS
AND
HOW TO SHINE AT EVERY ONE

SMART QUESTIONS TO ASK ABOUT THE STRUCTURE OF INTERVIEWS: THE SIX PHASES OF EVERY INTERVIEW

An interview is an interview is an interview—isn't it? Of course not. Even within a particular category of interview (i.e., employee/employer, information, networking, employment agency, etc.) each interview is unique and individual. Interviews are made up of the interaction between two human beings. There's no way to predict exactly how they'll go or what pattern they will follow.

But there is a logical sequence to all interviews. If you understand each of these phases, you'll come out of any interview situation a winner. The six components are:

- The Preparation
- The Opening
- The Body

- •The Tough Spots
- •The Closing
- •The Follow-up

THE PREPARATION

If you've been following the advice of the previous seven sections, you've already done most of the basic preparation. Before you even *think* about setting up any kind of interview, ask yourself these questions and construct a similar checklist:

- •Have I done a thorough self-examination?____
  - •Do I know what it is I'm looking for?____
  - •Have I prepared my Arsenal of Accomplishments?____
  - •Can I speak about myself in realistically positive terms, highlighting my strengths and putting the best spin on my weaknesses?____
  - •Have I made up my personal priority list?____
- •Do I have a basic overview of the industry in which I'm interested?____
  - •Do I have enough information about the company?____
  - •Do I have enough information about the inteviewer?___
- •Do I understand the concept of thinking like a boss?____
  - •Have I practiced simulated interviews?____
  - •Have I sharpened my communications skills?____
  - •Do I have a "packaging" checklist prepared to use before every interview?____
- •Do I know why people "buy"?____
  - •Have I practiced seeing and selling myself from an interviewer's perspective?____
  - •Do I believe in myself so that I can effectively sell what I have to offer?____

- •Have I practiced using questions as a powerful communications tool?____
  - •Do I know the difference between open and closed questions, and when to use each?____
  - •Do I know how to use clarifying questions to be sure I understand what's being asked of me?____
  - •Do I know how to be an active listener?____
  - •Have I practiced picking up clues in interview situations?____

SECRET STRATEGY NUMBER 13:
Thorough preparation is the cornerstone of
self-confidence and the foundation for making
a positive impression.

WHAT'S THE BEST WAY TO PRACTICE FOR AN UPCOMING INTERVIEW?

As every successful athlete, actor, musician, comedian, and salesperson knows, the only way to be prepared for "the big event" is to practice, practice, practice. Even before you go out on your first interview, you can practice the interview situation. Ask a friend or family member to role-play with you. And switch roles a few times—pretend you are the interviewer. See how you respond to various questions and comments, and what you would be looking for in an interviewee. This will help you in knowing what you need to do in order to prepare for your own interviews.

WHEN SHOULD I BEGIN MY PREPARATIONS?

Many people make the mistake of waiting until the last minute to prepare. You can make some preparations the morning of the interview, but most should start at least a week ahead. Here are some questions you can ask your-self to get this process going:

- *What is the purpose of this interview?* The ultimate purpose of every interview is to get a job. However, keep in mind the particular type of interview, and where you want it to lead. At an information inter-view, for example, your objective is to find out as much as possible about the industry, the company, and/or the individual in whom you are interested. At a personnel interview, your objective is to get in to see the person with the hiring authority. Knowing your objective beforehand not only helps you achieve the desired results, it also gives you a sense of purpose and confidence that definitely comes across to the interviewer.

- *What questions do I plan to ask?* Write your list of ques-tions on index cards that you can easily carry in your purse or briefcase. Even if you've asked questions throughout the interview, you're sure to forget one or two. When the interviewer says, "Is there anything else you'd like to ask?" you can reply, "I brought a short list of questions with me. Just let me check to be sure we've covered all of them." This shows the inter-viewer that you cared enough to prepare for the inter-view, that you're organized and pay attention to detail.

- *Have I got everything I need for the interview?* You should always take several clean copies of your résumé. If you're going for a networking interview, the interviewer might want a few copies so that he can pass them on to other contacts. The same may be true for an information interview. At this type of interview, you might also want to take notes. Be sure you have paper and pens. If you want to tape-record the interview, be sure to ask permission up-front. If it's all right, carry extra tapes and batteries with you.

If applicable, bring samples of your previous work. If you're a graphic artist or an advertising copywriter, for example, you may want to bring your portfolio as well as one or two samples you can leave with the interviewer.

- *How will I get there?* Call the company several days in advance, confirm the appointment date and time, and be sure you know where you're going. Ask for the best way to get there. If possible, travel the route before the actual interview day so you know how much time it will take. Have contingency plans set up so you'll know what to do if your car won't start, if there's a fire in the subway, or if the bus drivers go on strike.

- *What will I wear?* This should *never* be a last-minute decision. In your research, you should have found out about the corporate culture—is the company straitlaced and conservative? Is the atmosphere casual and offbeat? Find out, and dress appropriately. Remember, the interviewer wants to know if you'll fit in with the rest of the team. Being too conservative or too casual at an interview will certainly diminish your chances. Don't wear clothes that need to be adjusted when you stand up or sit down. If you wear jewelry, keep it simple and clank-free. Big bracelets or dangling earrings are taboo, since that type of jewelry can be enormously distracting.

THE OPENING

Many people say that the first five minutes of any interview are the most crucial, and that the decision of whether or not you will be hired is made in this short time span. This is probably not true (there are too many other factors at play), but first impressions can certainly help or hinder your chances of reaching your objective.

WHAT CAN I DO TO MAKE A POSITIVE FIRST IMPRESSION?

Here are six pointers to help you make a positive first impression:

1. *Make an entrance.* Arrive ten or fifteen minutes early if possible, but not earlier (you don't want to appear overanxious). As you are waiting to enter an interviewer's office, go over your list of questions and review your objectives for this interview.

   As you walk into the office look as though you would rather be there, about to speak to this particular person, than any other place in the world. Walk in with ease and purpose, and take a moment to collect yourself before you begin speaking.

2. *Make eye contact.* Your eyes are your most important physical feature, because they are crucial in establishing rapport. Make eye contact *before* you begin to speak. Don't stare at the other person, but make eye contact periodically during your entire visit.

3. *Watch your posture.* Sloppy posture conveys a lack of confidence and possibly a lack of discipline. It's surprising how many people neglect this aspect of their appearance. Don't sit on the edge of a chair; lean back and be comfortable without getting too casual. Maintaining good posture can elevate your state of mind and help you feel as confident and self-assured as you look.

4. *Don't hide behind your glasses.* Glasses with heavy

rims will hide your face and interfere with eye contact. Half-lens glasses give the unpleasant impression that you're looking down your nose at people. The next time you change your glasses, try the kind with large lenses and narrow frames. Stay away from strong tinting or light-sensitive glasses that darken in a brightly lighted room. You might want to opt for contact lenses.

5. *Control your hands.* Inexperienced interviewees are often nervous about what to do with their hands while they're speaking. Hands can take care of themselves if you know what *not* to do:

- Don't grip your briefcase, portfolio, or chair arms and hold on for dear life.
- Don't keep your hands in your pockets all the time or folded rigidly across your chest.
- Don't fiddle with your jewelry or your tie.

There are four ways in which you can use your hands to communicate ideas better: to emphasize shape, size, number, and direction. Practice gestures in front of a mirror—get a feel for what you are doing and what you look like.

6. *Smile.* Unless you're dealing with a life-or-death issue, smile naturally and often. It projects warmth and loosens up your facial muscles. Most people look better when they smile, and it makes interviewers more comfortable because you appear more natural and confident. A grim face isn't going to help you develop rapport with a prospective boss.

SHOULD I SPEAK FIRST IN THE INTERVIEW, OR SHOULD I WAIT FOR THE INTERVIEWER TO SAY SOMETHING?

Don't worry about exactly who speaks first—every interview starts out with a few seconds of "Hello" and "Nice to meet you." But you should try to ask the first question. You want to make an effective first impression, and you also want to take control immediately. Remember, the person who asks the question gains control.

Take a deep breath, and take a few seconds to look around you. Comment on the office environment—always in the form of a question, of course. You might say something like, "You have a spectacular view. Have you been in this office long?" Or, "I see you have several bowling trophies. Do you play often?"

WHAT'S THE BEST TYPE OF OPENING QUESTION TO ASK?

If you can find out something about the interviewer ahead of time, it gives you a distinct advantage. For example: "I saw in *Advertising Age* that you were just promoted to creative director last month. What do you feel has most contributed to your success here?" The interviewer can't help but be impressed (and flattered) that you have taken the time and effort to learn something about her.

If you've come through a recommendation, you could ask, "How do you and Daniel Tompkins know each other?" If you're on an information interview, you might start off with, "Thank you for seeing me. I know you're busy. How much time do we have to talk?"

THE BODY

There is one rule you must remember about interviews: there are no hard and fast rules about interviews. Every one is different. Most people are not professional interviewers; each interviewer has a style and a system all his own and will set up a format that is comfortable for him.

That's why preparation is so important. You won't know what the format is until you get there. If you've done your research and are prepared, the format of the interview shouldn't make any difference.

WHAT IS A TYPICAL INTERVIEW FORMAT?

There are basically three types of interviews. If an interviewer is very good (and not many of them are), she may suggest that you feel free to ask questions throughout the interview.

Someone else, who is less secure, might say, "I'm going to tell you all about the job. When I'm through, I'll ask you questions, and then you may ask any questions you have." This type of person usually talks so much, there is very little time left at the end for you to get a question in edgewise.

Then there are interviewers who don't set up any game plan, who start right in to interview. In that case, you should feel free to ask questions as they arise. If the interviewer is not comfortable with that, she will let you know.

SUPPOSE I DON'T LIKE THE FORMAT THE INTERVIEWER HAS SET UP?

You may choose to go along with the setup, or you may politely object. Even if the interviewer has stated that you should save your questions for the end, you can interrupt with, "Excuse me, do you mind if I ask one question here? There's something I'd like to clarify." The interviewer probably won't realize that you're changing the rules, and will be glad to explain what he or she meant.

DURING MY ROLE-PLAY INTERVIEW PRACTICE, MY PARTNER MENTIONED THAT I SOMETIMES GESTURED WILDLY WHEN ANSWERING HER QUESTIONS. WOULD THIS COUNT AGAINST ME IN AN INTERVIEW SITUATION?

Your gestures and mannerisms can help put interviewers on your side, or they can make people uncomfortable and even antagonistic. Here is a list of common gestures and how they are perceived:

DEFENSIVENESS:
Arms crossed on chest
Pointing index finger
Karate chops

REFLECTIVE:
Head tilted
Stroking chin
Peering over glasses

SUSPICION:
Arms crossed
Sideways glance
Rubbing eyes

OPENNESS AND COOPERATION:
Open hands
Leaning forward in chair
Unbuttoned coat
Tilted head

CONFIDENCE:
Hands on lapel of coat
Steepled hands

INSECURITY AND NERVOUSNESS:
    Chewing pencil or pen
    Rubbing thumb over thumb
    Biting fingernails
    Clearing throat
    Fidgeting in chair
    Poor eye contact
    Playing with hair

When you're practicing your interviewing skills, have friends or family members watch out for nervous habits or tics that might distract the interviewer's attention.

THE TOUGH SPOTS

Not every interview has tough spots. Some run along smoothly, come to a satisfying conclusion, and fulfill your objectives. Unfortunately, these interviews are the exceptions, not the rule. We all run into difficult situations from time to time: the phone keeps ringing throughout the interview, the secretary keeps popping her head in the door, the interviewer asks you a question for which you are not prepared, etc. If you run into a tough spot, don't panic. Use your common sense to deal with the situation. Even if you don't handle it perfectly, you can learn a valuable lesson so you'll know what to do should the situation arise again.

WHAT SHOULD I DO IF THERE ARE CONSTANT INTERRUPTIONS DURING MY INTERVIEW? IS IT BETTER TO IGNORE OUTSIDE INTERFERENCE, OR TO CONFRONT THE INTERVIEWER?

In any type of interview, you can usually ignore one or two interruptions. But if you've been sitting there for ten minutes and the interviewer has already taken three phone calls, you know his attention is divided, if not completely focused elsewhere. You can confront the situation without directly confronting the interviewer.

You might ask, "Would it be better for me to come back another time?" Or "Would you like me to leave the room when you get a phone call?" That way you bring attention to the situation (which the interviewer might not even realize is getting out of hand) without seeming annoyed or aggressive.

WHAT SHOULD I DO IF AN INTERVIEWER OFFERS ME SOMETHING TO EAT, DRINK, OR SMOKE?

In most cases, your best bet is to decline all offers. Even if you smoke, and so does the interviewer, wait until you get outside. If you're nervous, you may have difficulty lighting the cigarette, spill ashes on the carpet, or burn a hole in the chair.

Never take anything to eat (unless you're being interviewed over a meal). You want to be able to ask or answer a question at any time, and if you have food in your mouth, you could be in an embarrassing situation.

If you're thirsty, or your mouth is dry, you may accept an offer of something to drink (nonalcoholic), especially if the interviewer is drinking as well. This sometimes creates an informal atmosphere and helps you relax. If you do accept a drink, however, be sure there is a clear, uncluttered surface for you to put down the cup or glass. You don't want to take the chance of spilling anything onto important papers; nor do you want to be left juggling a glass in one hand while trying to open your briefcase with the other.

WHAT HAPPENS IF THE INTERVIEWER ASKS ME A QUESTION FOR WHICH I'M NOT PREPARED? OR WHAT IF I GET FLUSTERED AND CAN'T REMEMBER WHAT I'VE PRACTICED?

Don't panic. You don't have to answer every question when it's asked. You can always try a diversionary tactic: "That's a very good question, Mr. Sands, but would you mind if I asked you a question that just came to mind?" Or you might be more direct and say, "That's a tough question. I need time to think about my answer. Can we come back to it later?"

WHAT IF I'VE ALREADY ANSWERED A QUESTION, AND LATER REALIZE I DIDN'T ANSWER IT WELL, OR LEFT OUT AN IMPORTANT POINT?

Go back to it. Say, "Before we go on, I'd like to go back to an earlier question. Would that be all right?"

WHAT IF THE INTERVIEWER SEEMS TO BE WRAPPING UP AND I HAVEN'T TOUCHED ON ALL MY RELEVANT STRENGTHS?

Bring them up yourself; don't be shy. Say, "Before I leave, I'd like to bring up a subject we haven't yet covered, and that is my experience in supervising team projects. Let me give you a short example...."

WHAT IF I FEEL I'VE BOTCHED AN INTERVIEW FOR A JOB I REALLY WANT?

Be honest and direct. You might say, "I realize that this interview has not gone as well as I would have liked. Can you tell me what your concerns are so that I might allay your fears if at all possible?" Or you might want to press for a second interview: "Mr. Sands, have you ever wished for a second chance to make a better impression? I'd like that chance since I really want to work for you. Can we meet again next week?" You've got nothing to lose, and the interviewer will probably admire you for being courageous and forthright.

THE CLOSING AND THE FOLLOW-UP

Closing impressions are almost as important as the first five minutes. I remember interviewing someone for a position in my office a few years back. The interview had gone well, and I mentally put this young woman on my list of "possibilities." At the end of the interview, I asked, "Is there anything else you'd like to ask?" She answered, "Nope. I've heard enough. Guess I'll be hearing from you, huh?" I assume she didn't mean to come across as curt or as cavalier as she did, but that one closing remark make me think twice about hiring her. She did not get the job.

WHAT'S THE BEST WAY TO CLOSE AN INTERVIEW?

Remember that you are selling yourself at every interview. We'll go into "closing the case" fully in Section 17, when you'll learn how to actually ask for the job, but that's not the only aspect of closing the interview.

Just as you did at the beginning, take a deep breath and give yourself a few seconds to assess the situation. You might want to sum it up in a few sentences: "As I understand it, Mr. Sands, you are looking for someone who is X, Y, and Z. I know I have these qualities and can do a good job for you. Is there anything else you need to know about me?"

I KNOW I SHOULD FOLLOW UP EVERY INTERVIEW. BUT WHAT IF THE INTERVIEW DIDN'T GO SO WELL?

No matter how the interview went, let the interviewer know you appreciate the time spent. *Always* follow up with a note, a phone call, or an appropriate gift. Follow-up is critical—it is the one step most people do not take, and if you do, it can set you apart from a crowded, competitive field.

These six phases are part of every interview. The next six chapters will discuss various types of interviews you should learn to use to your advantage: the information interview, the networking interview, the employment-agency interview, the temporary-agency interview, the headhunter interview, and the personnel-department interview.

SMART QUESTIONS TO ASK ABOUT THE INFORMATION INTERVIEW

PICTURE THIS:

You've been a dental hygienist for twelve years. You're good at what you do, work for a well-known, well-respected dentist, and have reached the top of the pay scale for your field. But you're not happy. You're "tired of looking into people's mouths all day."

In your spare time you always read books about exotic lands and you've actually visited a few during your scheduled vacation times. You're pretty sure you'd like to move out of dental hygiene and "do something in travel." Frankly, though, you don't know much about the travel industry and have no idea how you would make such a change. What do you do first?

You go on information interviews.

WHAT IS AN INFORMATION INTERVIEW?

It is just what its name implies: an interview meant to provide you with facts, figures, opinions, impressions, etc., about the job or career in which you're interested. It's an investigative step in your job search; its purpose is not necessarily to get you an offer, or even a lead, for a job.

If you're changing from one field to another, are re-entering the work force after an extended absence, or are just coming into the job market, you may not know many details about the industry you're considering. If you go on information interviews, where the object is not necessarily to get a job offer, you can concentrate on filling in the gaps in your knowledge.

WHAT CAN I GAIN FROM INFORMATION INTERVIEWS?

Information interviews can provide you with more than facts. They can help you make decisions as to how and where you want to make a living. You can then proceed with your job search knowing:

- This is an industry that might offer you the kind of satisfaction that you've been seeking (or that this is *not* the right place for you, saving you years of frustration and wasted time).
- You can now back up your desire to enter this industry with the basic knowledge of how it works.
- You can confidentially proceed with the interviewing

process, knowing that you have the skills and qualities (or know how to obtain them) that are necessary to succeed in this field.

SECRET STRATEGY NUMBER 14:
Use information interviews to find out both the
positive and negative aspects of a job or industry.

MAKING CONTACT

HOW DO I GET TO THE PEOPLE WHO HAVE THE INFORMATION I NEED?

One way is to use your networking skills (see Section 10). Ask people you know if they know anyone in the field who might be able to help you. But be careful here—you don't want to "use up" your contacts or pester them too often, because you'll probably want to ask these same people for job leads.

You might ask a smart question like, "Right now I'm looking for people who can give me information about the travel industry. If I decide I do want to go into that field, would it be all right to contact you again?" Make each of your contacts a mentor, anxious and eager to help you again. Let them know how much you appreciate what they're doing for you.

DO I NEED TO KNOW THE PERSON OR HAVE A DIRECT REFERENCE TO GET AN INFORMATION INTERVIEW?

No, you don't. The best way to go about making contact with someone you don't know is to write to them directly. The most important point to remember while writing this letter is that *you're not asking, expecting, or implying that you're looking for a job.*

HOW CAN I WRITE AN EFFECTIVE LETTER?

The most successful letters include these five important points:

1. *Open with the reason you're contacting this particular person:* If you've been referred to this person, you might say, "Terry Brooks suggested that because of your expertise in the travel industry, you would be the perfect person from whom to seek advice." If you are contacting this person without a reference, you might say, "Your extensive experience and success in this field convince me that there is no one better qualified to give advice to newcomers."

2. *Include a brief summary of your background.* Let the potential interviewer know why you're interested, or think you might be qualified, for this field.

3. *Give the potential interviewer a hint of what you expect to gain from the interview.* For example, "I would like to get an insider's view of what the travel industry is like, how I can best use the skills I already have, and what training I might need to succeed in this field."

4. *Ask for a short meeting.* Let the interviewer know you will take up only about fifteen or twenty minutes of his time. Then, when you get to the meeting, it is up to the interviewer to give you more time (which is usually what happens).

5. *Extremely important! Include a statement in the letter that you do not expect that this interview will lead to a job offer.* You are seeking information only. Do not include or attach your résumé (you will bring it with you to the interview).

6. *Close the letter by stating that you will call on a specific date to arrange a meeting.*

Here is a sample of an effective letter:

September 10, 1993

Mr. Edward O'Toole
President
World Wanderings Inc.
1 Park Place
Anytown, USA

Dear Mr. O'Toole:

As the president of one of this city's largest travel agencies, your experience and success in the field convince me there is no one better qualified to give advice to newcomers.

I have been a dental hygienist for the past twelve years, honing not only my dental skills, but my communication and "people" skills as well. I am considering changing careers, and my love of travel has led me to explore this industry. Your advice concerning how I can best use the skills I already have and what training I might need to succeed in this field would, I am sure, prove invaluable.

Be assured that I am not asking you for a job. I

realize you are extremely busy, but I am seeking only fifteen to twenty minutes of your time. I will call you on September 16 to set up a meeting.

Sincerely,
Elane Miller

BE CLEAR ABOUT YOUR OBJECTIVE

There are three goals for information interviews:

1. To get valuable information about specific jobs and careers.
2. To make contacts within an industry.
3. To be remembered—in case a job opportunity should arise, or a referral come to mind.

WHAT IS THE MAIN OBJECTIVE OF AN INFORMATION INTERVIEW?

Your main objective is to get information. There are people who request an information interview with the idea that they will manipulate it into a job-seeking opportunity. This is not only deceptive, it can backfire. If the interviewer sees you as a deceptive person, you will have lost any possibility for future considerations.

This doesn't mean you should totally discount the possibility of getting a job interview out of the situation. You should always be prepared for such an eventuality. This happened to a friend of mine who obtained an information interview with the head of the training department of a large corporation. After one half hour the interviewer said, "I'm impressed with your background and your enthusiasm about training. Would you like to discuss the possibility of employment here?"

SAMPLE QUESTIONS

In an information interview, *you are the interviewer.* The person from whom you are seeking advice may ask you a few questions about your background and the reasons you want to enter a new field, but you will do most of the asking.

Therefore you must be fully and appropriately prepared. Write your questions down. Ask the interviewer if you can tape-record your conversation; that way you can listen to his or her advice at your leisure. If you don't have a tape recorder, or if the interviewer prefers not to be taped, be sure you take accurate notes. If you have contacted experts in the field, you will be getting information you can't get from any book.

Remember, however, that the answers you do get are only one person's perspective. Perhaps this person had a particularly difficult, or unexpectedly easy time entering the field. Perhaps she knows only one aspect of a broad industry. If you're considering various options within an industry, you'll probably want to set up several different information interviews to get an overview.

Here are some sample questions to ask, and suggestions about what you should be looking for in the answers:

WHAT DO YOU LIKE ABOUT THIS INDUSTRY?

Although the answer will be personal to your adviser, you want to know about the positive aspects of this industry. Are these the same things you would enjoy?

One of the things that I enjoy about my career as a speaker is the fact that I never know exactly what lies ahead—someone may call out of the blue tomorrow to ask me to come speak in Amsterdam in October, for example. Are you the type who enjoys the suspense and surprise, or are you looking for a more structured schedule?

On the other hand, if you were speaking to the head of an accounting firm, he might tell you that he loves numbers, and his favorite part of the business is dealing with numbers all day. You must then ask yourself if you would love dealing with numbers all day, or if that would be a turnoff for you.

WHAT DON'T YOU LIKE?

The same situation I described above about my business has its drawbacks. I don't know what the future holds, and sometimes that is a frightening concept. Although no job is secure nowadays, you may prefer to have a situation where you can follow a clear career path and collect a definite paycheck at the end of each week.

The accounting-firm president may say his least favorite part of the job is the incredibly long hours he must work. If you are someone who does not want, or is not able, to put in consistently long hours, this may not be a field that is right for you.

WHAT ARE SOME OF THE JOBS THAT ARE AVAILABLE IN THIS INDUSTRY?

If you're interested in the travel industry, for example, you may be familiar with the position of travel agent. But you may not know about other jobs within the industry, such as being a tour guide, or working within a large corporation arranging transportation for large meetings and conferences.

WHAT DO MOST PEOPLE LOOK FOR WHEN THEY HIRE IN THIS FIELD?

Of course, this will depend on the particular job you end up pursuing, but there are often characteristics that are important for the industry as a whole. You want to know what skills you need for this type of career. You want to know what's important to bosses in this field, and what kinds of personal characteristics employers admire. This will not only help you assess your own qualifications for this type of career, it will help you think like a boss when you get into actual job interviews in this field.

WHAT KIND OF TRAINING DO I NEED?

Do you need to go back to school? Do you need to take computer courses? Are there skills you can learn on the job? Do you need advanced knowledge of particular skills, or will the basics serve until you get more experience?

Try to get your adviser to be as specific as possible. For instance, if someone suggests that you should go back to school, ask if they know the best place to go. Are there schools that the industry holds in high regard? Are there schools that specialize in the kind of skills you'd need?

WHAT IS A TYPICAL DAY AT WORK LIKE FOR YOU?

This is an important question to ask. All of us have an unconscious tendency to glamorize our daily lives, make ourselves seem more important than we are, or gloss over the dreary details of the daily grind. If you ask your adviser to take you through a typical day, he'll have to include the good, the bad, and the ugly.

You might even want to ask if it would be possible for you to spend a day at your adviser's company to really see how things work. You would, of course, have to promise to keep out of everyone's way and not be a nuisance, but if you can get permission, you'll learn a lot more than you can through an interview.

HOW DID YOU GET INTO THE INDUSTRY?

There are two reasons for asking this question. One is that most people love to talk about themselves. If you're having any trouble getting your adviser to open up, a question like this will usually be a way to get him going. The answer will also allow you to gain from someone else's experience. Perhaps this person found an unusual route to get where she is, or made some mistakes along the way that you can avoid now that you know about them.

IS THERE A "TYPICAL" CAREER PATH FOR PEOPLE IN THIS FIELD?

If your adviser turns out to be the CEO's nephew, he may not have entered this industry along the same path as most people do. You want to know how most people get into the field, and what happens once they've gotten in.

In some large corporations, for instance, there are often set pathways to promotion; you start in one position and move up step-by-step until you reach the top. In other industries, it may be more beneficial to move from company to company in order to move ahead. Or the road to success may take a concerted self-marketing campaign, making it important for you to publish articles or become an officer in trade associations.

WHAT TYPE OF ADVANCEMENT OPPORTUNITIES ARE THERE?

How difficult is it to get ahead? Is the industry saturated right now, or is there a lot of room for advancement? Are there equal opportunities for women and minorities? How long does it usually take to move up in the company or get recognized in the field?

DO MOST PEOPLE WORK LONG HOURS OR A LOT OF OVER-TIME?

Again, the answer to this may be different for different jobs within an industry. But this question is especially important if you have restrictions on your time. If you're a single parent, and this is an industry where everyone works sixty-hour weeks, it may not be right for you. On the other hand, a field where people can accrue a lot of overtime, and the pay that goes with it, may be very attractive to you.

DOES THIS INDUSTRY, OR THIS JOB, HAVE A SEASONAL INFLUENCE?

An accountant, for example, is busiest during tax season. Winter is a slow period for construction. Retail does most of its business between Thanksgiving and Christmas. If you're thinking of going into retail management, and you're the kind of person who always goes skiing over the Christmas holidays, you'd better think again. You'll probably have to change your interest to tennis.

Also, in some industries, some employees get laid off during slow periods and hired again when things pick up. If you're just entering the field, you're likely to be one of the people scrambling for work in the off-season. Perhaps your adviser can tell you what other people do to get by during these times.

CAN YOU GIVE ME AN IDEA OF SALARY RANGES FOR ENTRY-LEVEL POSITIONS IN THIS INDUSTRY?

You can't expect your adviser to tell you exactly how much you'll be earning when you start out in this business. You're asking for a ballpark figure. Knowing the approximate salary you're likely to command as a newcomer may help you make a decision about changing careers. If the salary is way below what you've been making, you may not be able to make the change, at least not right away. On the other hand, if you've put away some of the money you've earned, you may be able to supplement a low-income job with your savings.

WHAT EFFECT DOES THE STATE OF THE ECONOMY HAVE ON THIS INDUSTRY?

No career is economy-proof; however, some are more affected than others. You want to find out if there have been large-scale layoffs in the industry recently, or hiring freezes. It could be difficult to start a new career in such a field. Conversely, an industry that is expanding, building new facilities, and/or diversifying may provide excellent opportunities to get in on a growth period.

WHAT DO YOU SEE AS THE GROWTH POTENTIAL FOR THIS INDUSTRY?

Is this an industry that's been growing steadily for many years? Is it a "fad" industry—one that's hot right now but may fade out tomorrow? Is the market for this industry's product or service shrinking or expanding? For example, products and services for the elderly have definite growth potential right now as the population continues to age. If you're interested in moving into a company or career that caters to this segment of the population, you can probably count on it having a high growth potential.

WHAT ABOUT MY BACKGROUND WOULD BE ATTRACTIVE TO EMPLOYERS?

To go back to the original premise, why would anyone in the travel industry want to hire someone who has twelve years of experience as a dental hygienist? Looking at a résumé alone, there probably isn't much there of interest to potential employers. However, your adviser may tell you to emphasize your ability to put people at ease in pressure situations, which could translate into your ability to handle travel clients who run into problems. She may also tell you to stress your familiarity with many exotic locations. These are both qualities that are valuable in the travel industry.

WHAT TYPE OF OBJECTIONS DO YOU THINK THEY WOULD HAVE?

Although you're not asking your adviser for a job, she'll probably be able to put herself easily into the mind-set of a prospective employer. She can tell you what she would think if you did approach her for a job— what reservations she might have. She might also be able to help you figure out ways to overcome those objections.

LOOKING AT MY RÉSUMÉ, WHAT SUGGESTIONS WOULD YOU HAVE FOR IMPROVEMENT?

Ask how you can improve your résumé in content and in appearance (or if you don't yet have one, what you should include or leave out). Is it at all enticing to someone in this field? Is there anything on it that would immediately invite rejection? Is the information clearly presented and easy to read? Does it look professional?

WHAT ASSOCIATIONS BEST REPRESENT THIS INDUSTRY?

If you have not already gotten this information from the library, your adviser should be able to tell you the names of the professional associations that serve this industry. Ask which ones she belongs to, and how she views the organization. Does she find it helpful? Does she think it serves its members well? Is she active in the association? Does she think being an association member is useful, helpful, or even necessary to get ahead in this industry?

ARE THERE TRADE NEWSPAPERS AND MAGAZINES I SHOULD KNOW ABOUT?

To which of these publications does your adviser subscribe? Are they helpful? Do they contain technical information, management advice, or just news and gossip? Has she ever published an article in any of the trade publications? Does she think this is a good way to get visibility in the industry?

HOW ARE JOBS IN THIS FIELD ADVERTISED?

Will you find classified ads in the local newspaper, or only in the trade publications? Do the industry associations have any type of placement assistance?

WHAT IS THE BEST WAY TO GO ABOUT FINDING UNADVERTISED JOBS?

Your adviser may be able to give you specific names and addresses in answer to this question, or may simply give you general advice about keeping your eyes and ears open. However, now that she knows you, and knows that you are considering going into this field, she may volunteer to keep her own eyes and ears open for you. In this way information interviews can be useful even if you feel you have a pretty good idea of what this industry is like. You're killing two birds with one stone here: getting inside information and making an important contact.

IS THERE ANYTHING WE HAVEN'T COVERED I SHOULD KNOW ABOUT?

You should ask this question, or one similar to it, at the end of every interview. Give your adviser a chance to review the conversation you've just had, and think about any important details he may have neglected to mention.

DON'T FORGET TO NETWORK

HOW DO I USE THIS INTERVIEW TO EXPAND MY CONTACT BASE?

Before you leave, ask your adviser if she knows of anyone else in the industry who might be able to give you information (especially if she is knowledgeable only about her limited area). Also, ask her to keep you in mind if she hears of any appropriate positions for you. Leave a copy of your résumé with her for future reference.

HOW CAN I KEEP THIS PERSON AS A CONTACT THROUGHOUT THE JOB SEARCH?

Keep objective number three for information interviews in mind: to be remembered in case a job opportunity should arise or a referral come to mind. *Always* follow up an information interview with a thank-you note. Let your adviser know how much you appreciate the time he took to see you, and how much you learned from your conversation. If you think it's appropriate, you might also want to send a small gift. Flowers or candy might be appropriate, or something that might appeal to a special interest of his. Do not go overboard; this is only a token of your appreciation.

Also, keep the adviser posted about your decision whether or not to go into the industry, and about your progress in locating a job.

* * *

The more you know about any industry, the more you'll know about what people in that industry are looking for and what qualifications you already possess. You can then tailor your approach in a job interview to stress those particular qualifications.

You can even quote your sources as authorities in the industry: "Edward O'Toole at World Wanderings says you need patience and logic to succeed in this industry. These are two of my strongest qualities."

Information interviews also serve as practice for job interviews, so that when you actually have a job offer at stake, you'll be prepared and confident of your interviewing abilities.

SMART QUESTIONS TO ASK ABOUT THE NETWORKING INTERVIEW

PICTURE THIS:

You're walking down a crowded street during rush hour. You literally bump into your old friend Tom. You exchange a few pleasantries. When Tom asks you "what's new?" you tell him that you're looking for work in the travel industry.

"Oh, great," says Tom. "My uncle runs a travel agency. If I can find his number, I'll give you a call. Got to run now . . . Good luck!"

Whether you know it or not, you just had a preliminary networking interview. Whether or not anything comes of this chance meeting is largely up to you.

*   *   *

SEEK AND YE SHALL BECOME CONNECTED

IS NETWORKING AN IMPORTANT SKILL FOR ME TO LEARN?

Statistics show that up to *80 percent of all new jobs are found through networking.* Remember the old saying "It's who you know that counts"? It is absolutely true. This doesn't mean that in order to get a job you must know someone who is in a position to hire you. Networking is like a chain reaction. You probably already know someone who knows someone who knows someone who can connect you to someone who is in a position to hire you. Everyone has contacts. Somewhere along the line, someone you talk to will put you in touch with someone who will offer you a job.

ARE THERE DIFFERENT TYPES OF NETWORKING INTERVIEWS?

Networking interviews can be formal (prearranged, with business contacts or acquaintances) or informal (via chance meetings or conversations with friends, family, etc.). A formal networking interview may take place in an office setting; an informal interview may take place anywhere at all.

WHAT KINDS OF NETWORKING LEADS SHOULD I BE PURSUING?

Any kind you can get.

SECRET STRATEGY NUMBER 15:
All networking leads are worth pursuing.

Not every lead will turn out to be productive, but you'll never know unless you take the time to find out.

The most farfetched situations usually turn out to be the most interesting. Katie, a friend of my daughter's, had been looking for work for about eight months. Then one day she was standing on line at a copy shop, waiting to have her résumé duplicated. When she got up to the counter, the woman who was copying her résumé said, "I see your background is in accounting. My father-in-law runs a small business and has been using the same accountant for years. The accountant is about to retire and my father-in-law was just complaining about having to look for a new one. Maybe you should give my husband a call so he can give you the number."

Katie called the husband, who said his father had just hired someone, but that his own business used a large accounting firm, and perhaps she should call there and see if they have any openings. Using the husband's name, Katie called the president of the accounting firm, landed an interview, and was eventually offered a job.

WHEN SHOULD I BE NETWORKING?

All the time. Even if you are currently employed, with no immediate plans of changing jobs, practice your networking skills. You never know when your situation might change.

Of course, you should be networking constantly when you're looking for a job. You may feel shy or embarrassed to tell people you're unemployed, especially if you have been laid off or fired. Being out of work, however, particularly in this economic climate, is nothing to be ashamed of. Many people are facing the same situation.

That's why it's more important than ever to network. When the competition gets tougher, the number of people doing the basics—answering ads and sending out résumés—increases dramatically. Fewer people, however, realize the importance of networking—and even fewer actually do it. The sooner you start, the sooner you can get your network working for you.

HOW DO I KNOW WHICH NETWORKING CONTACTS WILL TURN OUT TO THE BE THE BEST LEADS?

There's no way to predict who among your contacts will produce the best leads; therefore you should contact everyone. This includes:

Friends	Your lawyer
Family	Your hairdresser
Old business acquaintances	Your insurance agent
College alumni	Your accountant
College professors	Club members
Your doctor	Association members
Your dentist	Civic leaders
	Everyone you know

HOW MANY LEADS SHOULD I EXPECT TO GET FROM MY NETWORKING CONTACTS?

Don't expect everyone you contact to come up with a lead or a name for you. According to Bernard G. Ramos's book *Job Hunters,* "You may expect one in four networking interviews will produce anything in the way of a job opportunity. The other three may yield valuable advice or contacts. You may also expect one in eight of your networking interviews to lead to a job offer." That means one quarter of your networking efforts will result in an actual job lead, and one eighth will result in a job offer.

IMPROVING THE ODDS

You can improve these numbers if you take a systematic approach to networking. Keep a networking notebook. Make a list of the different reasons you might have for networking, and the people you know who might fit those needs.

Your networking notebook might look something like this:

FAMILY, FRIENDS, ACQUAINTANCES

Is there anyone I know (don't forget distant relatives) who works in my field of interest?

_____

_____

If I don't know how to get in touch with that person, who does?

_____

_____

Do I know anyone who is an excellent networker?

_____

_____

(Get these people to help you network—they'll love it!)

Have I let everyone know I'm looking for a job? Did I tell my:

Friends ____	Family ____
Doctor ____	Lawyer ____
Dentist ____	Accountant ____
Neighbors ____	Former employers ____
Colleagues ____	Club members ____
Hairdresser ____	Insurance agent ____

Association members ____
Sport team members ____
College alumni and professors ____

SUPPORT GROUPS:

Are there any people around me who are "in the same boat"?

_____

_____

Have I done any favors for friends? Who are they?

_____

_____

_____

Which of my friends and colleagues recognize and appreciate my skills and accomplishments? (These are people who are most likely to take an active role in your networking process, and will give you the best recommendations.)

_____

_____

_____

Additional Names:

_____

_____

INSIDE SOURCES:

Who knows the most about my field of interest?

_____

_____

_____

Have I contacted:

Association presidents _____

Trade-publication editors or reporters _____

Experts or high achievers in the field _____

Do I know anyone who can put me in touch with these people?

_____

_____

Do I know anyone who can provide guidance or help me figure out what my next action should be?

_____

_____

If I don't know that person, do I know someone who does? (Most people enjoy helping, as long as you call at a convenient time and have specific questions in mind.)

_____

_____

_____

Additional Names:

_____

_____

FUTURE POSSIBILITIES:

Who are the people in my field of interest I'd most like to meet? (Someone I heard at a conference, someone a friend or colleague spoke highly of, etc.)

_____

_____

_____

How can I get in touch with these people?

_____

_____

_____

Are there any organizations I can join that will put me in contact with the kinds of people I want to meet?

Associations _____

Business clubs _____

Social clubs _____

Charity organizations _____

Are there any events I can attend where I may be able to make contacts?

Annual meetings _____

Conferences _____

Seminars _____

Classes _____

Do I know anyone, or is there anyone I want to know, who can make me think, who will challenge me to grow?

_____

_____

_____

How can I find these people? (Networking is very much like solving a puzzle—finding one clue leads you to the next and the next. One contact refers you to another, who refers you to another, until you find

that one contact who will provide you with the solution you need.)

_____

_____

_____

HOW CAN I USE NETWORKING TO IMPROVE THE ODDS OF GETTING THE INTERVIEWS I WANT?

Remember Secret Strategy Number 2: Be active, not
reactive. This is one of the most important principles of
the entire job-search process. You must take an active
role every step of the way. You can't just sit back and
wait for interviews to come to you; you must go after the
interviews you want. You can't just answer questions;
you must ask some yourself. And you can't hope that
other people will spread the word that you need a job;
you must get out there and do it yourself.

Perhaps the most valuable asset of networking is that
it is by nature an *active* process. It helps you to help
yourself; nobody else can network for you.

JUST WHAT DO YOU MEAN BY BEING ACTIVE?

Remember meeting Tom on that crowded street? He
said that his uncle runs a travel agency, and that if he
could find his number, he'd give you a call. Then he said
"Good luck!" and took off in the other direction.

What would you do in this situation?

    a) Ignore Tom because he's a little flaky and his
       uncle probably is, too?
    b) Assume Tom was just being polite, and would
       only be annoyed if you called?

    c) Wait for him to call with his uncle's number?
    d) Call Tom in a week or two and ask him if he has found the number?
    e) Call Tom the following day, and tell him if he knows the name of the travel agency, you'll be glad to look up the number?

If your reaction was not to call, think again. Tom may be busy, but if he offered to look for his uncle's number, he probably won't mind if you call. And even if he can't find the number, or says he's too busy to look, he may come up with another name that might be helpful to you.

If you answered "e," you're a true networker. People usually have good intentions—they intend to keep their promises about supplying you with names and numbers. But they get involved in their work, they get distracted, or they simply forget. It's up to you to call and remind them.

CONDUCTING THE NETWORKING INTERVIEW

ONCE I GET A NETWORKING CONTACT ON THE PHONE, WHAT DO I DO?

If you did call Tom in the scenario above, would you just get his uncle's name and number and then hang up? That's what most people do. But in order to make networking an efficient process, you need to get more information.

You need to interview your networker. First, ask your networker if he has a few minutes to spare. If he says he's busy, ask if you can speak with him at another time, and find out a good time to call back.

You want to get as much information as you possibly can about the person (and/or the company) your net-

worker has recommended. He may not have all the
answers for you, but every answer he does have will be
of great help. Here are some of the questions you may
want to ask:

- *What is the correct spelling of the contact's name?* If
  you're planning to write to the contact, you must
  know the proper spelling. Even if you don't write to
  set up an interview, at some point you may want to
  send a résumé or a thank-you note.
- *What is the correct pronunciation of the contact's
  name?* My name is Dorothy Leeds. An easy enough
  name to pronounce, you would think. But people
  have called my office asking for Ms. Lee, Ms. Led,
  Ms. Leader. I even had one job applicant call and ask
  for Ms. Tree! I would never consider hiring that person, no matter how qualified she turned out to be!
  Ask your networker for the correct pronunciation
  and write it down phonetically so that you'll be sure
  to remember how to say it.
- *Can I use your name when I call or write to this contact?* If it is at all possible, you want to be able to say
  you were "recommended by . . ." A referral always
  makes you stand out from the crowd; it makes you
  more of a known quantity. It may also help you get
  through on the phone—if the secretary hears a
  name with which she is familiar, she's much more
  likely to connect you with her boss.
- *What is your relationship with the contact?* There are
  two reasons for asking this question. First, you want
  to find out if your networker has any clout or influence with the contact person. If the contact is your
  networker's mother, close relative, or best friend,
  your networker may have some influence. If the contact and the networker are close business associ-

ates, that's even better. If the contact is someone your networker has met once or twice, or is someone your networker has only heard of or read about, your networker may not have any influence.

Second, you want to know how to approach the contact. If your networker is well known to the contact, you could say, "Your nephew Tom recommended I call," or "Tom Smith from Acme Hardware recommended I call." If the contact is barely acquainted with the networker, or doesn't know him personally, you may not choose to mention his name at all.

- *What can you tell me about this person?* If your networker knows the person well, she may be able to give you some insights into his character, his personality, and/or his management style. If you're told that the contact is always very busy, has a serious, brusque manner, and likes to get right down to business, you'll know what to expect, and how to respond, when you call. On the other hand, your networker may say, "Oh, just give John a call anytime. He's got a great sense of humor, he's always looking for new people, and he's never too busy to help someone out." Obviously, your approach to John would be different.

- *What is the company like?* Any information you can get prior to calling will be of use to you. Once again, what you know about the company can help you determine the best approach to take. If the company is staid and conservative, you may be better off writing a formal letter of introduction before you call. If the corporate culture is more casual, a phone call may suffice.

- *Would it be possible for you to call or write first, to let the contact know I will be calling?* In sales there are two approaches to potential customers. One is the "cold call" and the other is the "referred lead." A cold call means that you are calling someone you don't know; someone who has in all likelihood never heard of you or your product or service. A referred lead means that you are calling someone who has been recommended to you, or someone you know has a particular interest in your service or product. Every salesperson greatly prefers the referred lead.

Having someone call or write first prepares your contact for your call, and gives you a referred lead. This is also another way to help you get past the protective secretary (see Section 16) by enabling you to say, "Mr. Jones is expecting my call."

- *When do you think you would be able to make this call or write this letter?* You don't want to call your contact before the networker has had a chance to do her part. If she can't give you a specific time, call back the following week and ask if she's sent the letter yet, or if she's had a chance to call the contact for you. If she hasn't, she'll probably get right on it so you don't have to call again. If your networker is busy, or helping you is a low priority (although her intentions are good), offer to write the letter for her (on her letterhead, of course). Then all she has to do is sign it. That's being active!

- *Have you ever recommended anyone to this person before?* If she has and it's worked out well, this could be to your advantage. If she has and nothing ever came of it, or if it worked out badly, you may decide not to take advantage of this particular lead, or not to use this networker's name.

- *Is there anyone else you can recommend I contact?* It never hurts to keep on networking!

Your networker may not be able to answer all of these questions. That's okay. Once you've gotten a name and phone number, any other information is gravy.

DON'T FORGET THE FOLLOW-UP

WHAT'S THE BEST WAY TO FOLLOW UP A NETWORKING INTERVIEW?

The hard-and-fast rule that applied to information interviews applies to networking interviews as well: always follow up an interview with a thank-you note. Let your networker know how much you appreciate the time he took to see you or speak with you. Write the letter immediately while the contents of the interview are still fresh in both of your minds.

WHAT SHOULD I INCLUDE IN THE LETTER?

Recap what went on in the interview. Tell the interviewer you will be contacting Mr. Smith and Mr. Jones, as she suggested. If you have already taken action on a referral, include that information in your letter. You might say, "Thank you so much for advising me to contact Virginia Spencer. I sent her a letter this morning using your name and requesting an appointment."

Keep your networker posted about your progress; be sure to let her know how your interview goes. If you end up getting a job offer, you might want to send your networker another thank-you note or a small gift.

SECRET STRATEGY NUMBER 16:
The object of a networking interview is to be remembered. You want your networker to keep

**thinking about you, thereby increasing
the possibility that he or she may come up
with some other contacts for you.**

Practice your networking skills whenever possible. Keep the statistics in mind: *80 percent of the available jobs are obtained through networking*. That should make it very clear just how important networking is to your job-search process.

SECTION 11

SMART QUESTIONS TO ASK ABOUT THE EMPLOYMENT-AGENCY INTERVIEW

Do you ever think, "Getting a job is a lot of hard work. I wish there was someone out there who could help me find what I'm looking for"? The good news is, there are people out there who can help. The bad news is, you have to be careful who you turn to or you just might get ripped off.

Again, you must take an active role. Thousands of people do get jobs through employment agencies—but if you want to be sure you'll be treated like a professional and sent out for the kinds of jobs you want, research the agencies in your area.

It's the people in every agency who make the difference. I was very fortunate, in writing this book, to have found several people who were willing and able to answer some of my questions about the different types of agency interviews. In this section, Jill Rosenfeld, Employment Manager at Mademoiselle Personnel Network in New York City, was most knowledgeable and helpful.

HOW AN AGENCY WORKS

I'VE HEARD SEVERAL UNPLEASANT STORIES ABOUT EMPLOYMENT AGENCIES. WHY DO THEY HAVE SUCH BAD REPUTATIONS?

The reason is this: Employment agencies work on commission. If they get you a job, the company that hires you pays them a fee. If you don't get a job, they get nothing. Therefore it's to the employment agency's bene-fit to get you a job—any job, whether it's the right job for you or not. Many unscrupulous agencies have pres-sured people into taking jobs for which they were not at all suited.

Happily, there are many excellent firms with coun-selors who really care about their applicants and try their best to match applicants' needs and desires with the jobs they have available. You may have to shop around until you find an agency you feel is right for you.

WHAT CAN I DO TO ENSURE THAT I GET THE MOST OUT OF DEALING WITH AN EMPLOYMENT AGENCY?

There are several steps you can take, including:

- *Make sure you are dealing with a reputable firm.* Call the Better Business Bureau and find out if there are any complaints against an agency you are considering.

- *Call personnel or the human-resources departments of large companies in your field of interest* and ask them which agencies they use.
- *Ask your counselor at the employment agency for the names of personnel managers with whom they work* so you can call for a reference.
- *Look for an agency that has been in business for a number of years,* and a counselor that has been at that agency for at least one year.
- *Always take an active role in the process.* Ask your counselor questions. Don't be afraid to say no. If a particular job or interview situation doesn't appeal to you, it's okay to refuse. A good agency will try to place you in jobs for which you are well suited. If you do not feel this is true, try another agency.
- *Don't rely solely on employment agencies to help you get a job.* Use your own networking skills and all other resources available to you.

WHAT TYPES OF JOBS DO EMPLOYMENT AGENCIES USUALLY HANDLE?

In general, employment agencies concentrate on supplying office-support staff. They usually place recent college graduates, up through $50,000 executive assistants. They may have some middle-management positions, but anything above that is usually handled by an executive search firm (see Section 13).

HOW DOES AN EMPLOYMENT AGENCY FIND OUT ABOUT AN AVAILABLE POSITION?

If there is an opening at a large company, someone from

personnel or human resources usually calls the employ-ment agency. If it's a small company, the call usually comes from an office manager, or directly from the person who's doing the hiring. Often, a company will work exclu-sively with a particular counselor at an agency, so if you're interested in working at a particular company, ask if there is a counselor there who handles that account.

WHAT IS THE EMPLOYMENT AGENCY TOLD ABOUT THE JOB?

It depends upon the client. Some personnel people are skilled at giving job specifications and will give the employ-ment counselor information on everything from job responsibilities to dress code. There are other clients that call the agency and say nothing more than "I need a secretary."

In general, clients provide information on what they're looking for in terms of experience, education level, skills, even personality. For instance, the personnel executive may let the agency know that this boss is someone who's difficult to work for, and they need someone who can work in that atmosphere. They might include information about whether or not the job requires a lot of overtime, if it's fast-paced or high pressure, or if it's a smoking envi-ronment. They always give a salary range.

A good corporate personnel executive will give the employment agency as much information as he or she possibly can. The more information the agency has, the better the agency's ability to make a perfect match.

HOW ARE EMPLOYMENT-AGENCY JOBS ADVERTISED?

The agency may run a single ad for a particular job, or they may run a large ad featuring several different available positions. All ads that are run through agencies are legally required to say so.

It's important to note that these ads are usually written by copywriters trained to make the jobs sound as enticing as possible. The agency may have 150 jobs available, but they choose 10 or 15 of the best jobs to advertise. Don't be misled by ads that offer glamorous, high-paying jobs. An ad that reads "Work for the Stars" may have you typing invoices for a company that makes telescopes.

WHAT TYPE OF INFORMATION IS CONTAINED IN THE ADS?

Ads are expensive, so they contain only the barest of job descriptions, which includes the industry (i.e., advertising, banking, etc.), the skills required (i.e., 50 wpm, knowledge of particular software, etc.), and some responsibilities. The ad may mention desired educational level, and generally includes a salary range.

HOW DO I CONTACT AN EMPLOYMENT AGENCY? DO I CALL FOR AN APPOINTMENT OR JUST WALK IN?

This depends on the agency, but most use both methods. It's a good idea to call first to make sure the job you're interested in is still available, and to get a general impression of the professionalism of the agency. If the person who answers the phone is rude or does not supply you with the information you need, you may want to look elsewhere.

IF I CALL FOR AN APPOINTMENT, WILL I BE PRESCREENED?

Again, it depends on the agency. Some will simply tell

you to come in and fill out an application. The better agencies do some prescreening on the phone. For instance, an agency may run an ad for a secretarial or administrative-assistant position in the publishing field. Often, they'll get editors calling about the job. Or if the job is for a fashion magazine, models will call. A good agency will say, "Do you understand that this is a secretarial position, and that you need secretarial experience?" They may then say, "This particular position doesn't seem appropriate for you. But if you'd like to come in and talk about other positions, please do."

SUPPOSE I CALL TO ASK FOR AN APPOINTMENT. WHAT SHOULD I BE ASKING ON THE PHONE?

If you're calling in response to a particular ad, you should ask for pertinent details about the job. Do not expect to go into depth about it, however. If you're still interested after this preliminary phone call, you can find out more details when you go into the agency. You might ask questions like:

- *What type of position is it?* Some agencies run misleading ads. They may use a job "title" that doesn't give you much of a clue as to what the job is really like. Is it a secretarial position? Is it an administrative position? What does that "title" really mean?
- *What kind of skills are you looking for?* You want to know if you have the required skills, or if not, how important those skills are to the job. For instance, the job may require knowledge of a specific computer-software program. If you don't have experience on that program, but are proficient on a similar program, that may be acceptable.

- *Is the advertised job in fact available?* Another reason for the bad reputation of employment agencies is that they sometimes run ads that are "come-ons." These are ads for great jobs that were available once upon a time, but were filled long ago. You don't want to go into an agency expecting to interview for the job of your dreams only to be told that job no longer exists.
- *Is this an employment agency?* Although it is legally required that agencies identify themselves in their advertising, many have found ways to get around it. If you're not sure, ask. If the ad seems to be deceptive, don't use this agency.
- *When can I expect to be sent on an interview?* No one can guarantee that you will be sent on an interview immediately. But there is always the possibility that you will be sent on one directly from the agency office—therefore you'll need to be prepared. Dress as if you were going on a job interview, and be sure to bring several copies of your résumé along with you.
- *Do you charge a fee?* Be leery of any agency that asks you for money. They may say the fee covers helping you rewrite your résumé, or guarantee you a job if you pay up front. Don't do it. Reputable agencies are paid by their clients, not by the people who come in to apply for jobs.

SHOP FOR AN AGENCY YOU LIKE

IS IT BETTER TO WORK WITH A LARGE AGENCY OR A SMALL AGENCY?

Many people feel that large agencies are like factories, that they don't have as much time as the smaller agencies do to devote to each applicant. That may be true, but a large agency will probably have more available jobs to offer you.

SECRET STRATEGY NUMBER 17:
Shop around for an employment agency you like; choose the agency in which you feel the most comfortable. Remember that any agency is only as good as the counselor with whom you work.

IF I DON'T LIKE THE PARTICULAR COUNSELOR WITH WHOM I'M WORKING, SHOULD I ASK FOR ANOTHER COUNSELOR?

There are hundreds of employment agencies in existence today. When you look for an agency, you should be looking for a counselor. A good employment counselor is part baby-sitter, part parent. It's almost like looking for a therapist—keep looking until you find one you connect with. If you can connect with a counselor, he or she is much more likely to find you the job you want.

IF I DO ASK FOR ANOTHER COUNSELOR, WILL IT BE HELD AGAINST ME?

In most agencies, it will not be held against you if you have a good reason to want to change counselors. Most agencies would rather move someone than lose someone.

WHAT HAPPENS WHEN I GO IN TO THE AGENCY?

Usually, you are first asked to fill out an application. Sometimes you will be tested for your skills immediately;

sometimes you will be interviewed first and then tested. If you have an appointment with a specific counselor, your application goes directly to that counselor. If you come in without an appointment, your application goes to the next available counselor.

WHAT INFORMATION IS INCLUDED IN AN APPLICATION?

A typical application asks for your name, address, level of education, languages, computer skills, references, and experience. You are usually asked to attach your résumé to the application. When filling out the application, never write "see résumé" even though the information is the same. Counselors are not just looking at the information on your application; they're also looking to see if your handwriting is legible, and if you can follow directions. Also, your application may go in your permanent file without your résumé.

QUESTIONING THE COUNSELOR

As in every interview we talk about, you should ask as many questions as you answer. Ask questions about the counselor herself, and about every interview she sends you out on. A good counselor will cover much of the information before you ask. However, everyone is human. The counselor may forget to tell you about an important detail. Bring a list of questions with you to the interview. This will not only give you the information you need, it will serve as good practice for the actual job interview.

You can, and should, be frank with your counselor. If you're nervous about interviewing, let her know. If you're not sure how to answer a question you think a potential boss will ask you, discuss it with your counselor. She should be glad to help you hone your interviewing skills. (She may be busy, however; don't expect that she can devote big chunks of time to helping you practice. Ask her for advice about practicing with friends and family.) Remember, she only gets paid if you get a job, so it's to her benefit to see that you are well prepared. Here are some of the questions you should be asking your counselor:

WHAT IS YOUR OWN BACKGROUND? HOW LONG HAVE YOU BEEN WITH THIS AGENCY?

You want to try to work with a counselor who has been with the agency for at least a year. If the counselor has been there awhile, she's probably very familiar with the needs of her clients, and what types of applicants match their needs best. If the counselor has changed agencies frequently, find out why.

DO YOU SPECIALIZE IN ANY PARTICULAR AREA?

Larger agencies often have counselors who specialize in particular industries. For example, they may have one counselor who places people in advertising jobs, another who places people in the financial industry, and another who deals mainly with high-tech companies. Be sure you're with a counselor who knows about jobs in your area of interest.

HOW DO YOU WORK WITH YOUR APPLICANTS? DO YOU CALL ME? DO I CALL YOU?

You want to know how the system works. Should you check in with the counselor every day to see if he has any interviews for you? Every other day? Or should you wait for him to call? (Don't wait too long. If you don't hear anything for several days, call anyway.)

WHAT CAN YOU TELL ME ABOUT THE COMPANY TO WHICH YOU'RE SENDING ME?

Is it a large company or a small one? If it is a large company, how large is the department in which you'd be working? Let the counselor know if you have a preference for one or the other. You may enjoy the energy and politics of a large corporation, or you may prefer to work in a more "family" type atmosphere. Ask the counselor to tell you her impressions of the corporate culture. Ask about the stability of the company, and how long they've been in business. Also ask the counselor where you can find out more information about the company; she may be able to help you get an annual report or a company brochure.

WHO WILL BE INTERVIEWING ME?

One of the disadvantages of an employment agency is that it is twice removed from your main objective—connecting with the person who has the power to give you a job. You want to talk directly with the person for whom you would be working. Using an employment agency, you must first speak with an employment counselor, who *may* send you to the personnel department, who *may* then send you in to see the potential boss. On the other hand, an employment agency may know about a job that has not been advertised, and send you out on an interview before it becomes widely known.

CAN YOU TELL ME ABOUT THE PERSON FOR WHOM I WOULD BE WORKING?

In most cases, the counselor doesn't know the potential boss. She probably got her information from the personnel executive who called in the job. However, any information you can get will be helpful to you. The counselor will usually be able to tell you at least if the boss is a high-pressure dynamo or has a more laid-back style of management.

WHAT IS THE CLIENT LOOKING FOR?

When the personnel executive called the agency, he gave the counselor an idea of the type of person he was looking for to fill this job. The counselor should be willing to share this information with you so that you can judge whether or not you fit the bill. For instance, they may be looking for someone who is extremely organized and detail-oriented. If these are not your strong points, you want to know so that you can: a) let the counselor know you'd rather not apply for this job, or b) discuss with your counselor ways of handling this subject so that you emphasize other strong qualities that will make up for your lack of organization.

WHAT BENEFITS DOES THE COMPANY OFFER?

One of the advantages of going through an employment agency is that you can ask your counselor questions you shouldn't ask an employer on a first interview. If the number of vacation days is important to you, for example, you can usually find this out in advance from the employment counselor.

WHAT SHOULD I WEAR TO THIS INTERVIEW?

The counselor should be familiar with the general atmosphere of the company. You should know if you need to wear very conservative attire, or if something more casual (but always professional) will do.

WHAT IS THE TIME OF THE INTERVIEW AND THE ADDRESS? DO I ASK FOR ANYONE IN PARTICULAR WHEN I GET THERE?

The counselor will probably tell you these details right up front, but you should always double-check to make sure you've written everything down correctly.

WHAT QUESTIONS SHOULD I BE ASKING AT THIS INTERVIEW?

Your counselor should be willing to practice with you. She wants you to do a good job. You might read her a list of questions you've prepared to take with you, and see if she has anything to add or delete.

CAN YOU HELP ME WITH MY RÉSUMÉ?

A good counselor should look over your résumé and recommend changes if necessary. She may recommend that you customize your résumé for a particular job. If the counselor does recommend changes, be sure you ask why and exactly how she would fix it so that you can take advantage of her advice when you go on other interviews.

DO YOU SEE ANY AREAS IN MY BACKGROUND THAT MIGHT CAUSE OBJECTIONS? IF SO, HOW SHOULD I HANDLE THEM?

If you have less experience than the client is looking for, or have had a number of different jobs in the past few years, or are moving from one industry to another, the client may have some reservations about hiring you. Your counselor should be experienced in dealing with these kinds of perceived shortcomings, and help you come up with ways to answer any objection that might arise.

WHAT HAPPENS AFTER THE INTERVIEW? DO YOU CALL THE COMPANY TO SEE HOW I DID? DO I CALL? DO I FOLLOW UP?

Usually, the counselor will get feedback from the personnel executive shortly after the interview (sometime that day or the day after). Find out if you should call the counselor or if she will call you when she hears (it's always better for you to call; then you're in control and don't have to sit and wait for the phone to ring). If the interview did not go well, ask the counselor what went wrong and how you can improve for next time. Most counselors recommend that the only follow-up you should do yourself with the personnel executive is to send a thank-you note. Send it immediately after your interview; hand-deliver it if possible (leave it with the receptionist).

WITH WHOM DO I DISCUSS SALARY?

When you use an employment agency, salary is usually discussed with your counselor—not with the personnel executive or the potential boss. Initially, the agency will give you a salary range. The counselor may say, "This job pays from $26,000 to $28,000." Whether or not you get the high end of the range usually depends on the amount of experience you have. Of course, you would prefer to get $28,000, if possible. But don't expect to go much higher. Remember that the counselor works on commission. If it's possible to get you more money, she'll certainly try— the more money you make, the more money she makes.

Employment agencies have their good and bad points. However, a reputable agency with experienced counselors can be a welcome boon to your job search.

SMART QUESTIONS TO ASK ABOUT THE TEMPORARY-AGENCY INTERVIEW

PICTURE THIS:

For the past five years you've been a word processor in a medium-size law firm. You're thinking about going back to school and starting a career in investment banking. Although you've done research into the field, and it seems to fulfill your criteria for a satisfying career, you'd love to get an insider's view of what the banking biz is really like. How can you explore this industry before you make an all-out commitment to it?

You can go the temporary route.

In years past, the perception was that people took temporary work because they couldn't find, or hold, a permanent job. But in this tough economy, working temp is looked on as a smart move by many people. If you're having a difficult time getting a permanent job, tempo-

169

rary work may be just what you need to tide you over.

According to Charles Handy's book *The Age of Unreason,* "By the end of the century . . . only one half of all paid workers will be in what, today, we would call 'proper' jobs. The other half will be self-employed, part-time workers or temporary workers."

Rachel Philipp, Director of Internal Operations for Madamoiselle Temporary Services in New York, was invaluable in providing information for this section.

HOW A TEMPORARY AGENCY WORKS

WHO PAYS THE TEMPORARY AGENCY'S FEES?

Temporary agencies work much the same way employment agencies do: they get paid by the companies that hire them, not by the people for whom they get jobs.

WHAT KINDS OF JOBS DO TEMPORARY AGENCIES USUALLY PROVIDE?

Temporary agencies most often deal in office-support jobs—anything from a mailroom clerk to a messenger on up to an executive secretary. Some specialize in book-keeping and finance, and some now have desktop-publishing divisions.

HOW DO I KNOW IF DOING TEMPORARY WORK IS THE RIGHT WAY FOR ME TO GO?

Not so long ago, there were only two types of people who did temp work: people who couldn't get a regular job, and artists, writers, and actors, who needed to make some money while pursuing their "real" careers. Now all kinds of people do temp work, for all kinds of reasons.

Signing up with a temporary agency may be particularly good for you if you are:

- still in school and are looking for work during the summers and vacations
- just out of school, looking for your first job, and have little or no office experience
- not sure what you would like to do and want to get a taste of a variety of fields
- changing careers and want to be sure you're heading in the right direction
- looking for part-time work or flexible scheduling

WHY DO COMPANIES HIRE TEMPORARY WORKERS?

Companies have traditionally hired temp workers to help them out when they had a temporarily heavy work load, or to fill in for full-time employees who were out sick for a day, on vacation, or on maternity leave. In this economy, the temporary worker has become more important than ever.

Many companies are saving money by using long-term temporary workers instead of permanent employees. That way they do not have to pay the temps' health benefits and unemployment insurance, and do not have to offer vacation time or pay. There are some temporary agencies that are now offering limited benefits to make up for this.

WHAT ARE THE ADVANTAGES OF DOING TEMP WORK?

The main advantage of this kind of work is that it gives you near-total freedom about when and where you work. If you have school-age children, for example, you can work when they're in school and stay at home when they're on vacation. Or if you're going to school yourself three days a week, you can work the other two days. Many people in the arts find that temporary work keeps them afloat when other work is hard to find.

The other advantage is that you can use temp work to "check out" a company or industry to find out if you would like to pursue a career in that area.

WHAT ARE THE DISADVANTAGES OF THIS KIND OF WORK?

The main disadvantage is that, in most cases, you get no benefits, such as health insurance. And you get paid only for the days you work, which means no sick days or paid vacations.

Temp work is not for everyone. Some people do get long-term temp assignments, and are on the same job for months, or even years, at a time. Most people, however, are offered daily or weekly jobs. That means you are constantly changing from one job to another, working in unfamiliar surroundings with people you don't know, and trying to adjust to a new company's work style in only a few hours. Unless you are comfortable with rapid change, temp work can be very stressful.

HOW DOES THE TEMPORARY AGENCY FIND OUT ABOUT AN AVAILABLE POSITION?

As in the case of the employment agency, it depends on the size of the company. If there is an opening at a large company, someone from personnel or human resources usually calls the agency. If it's a small company, the call usually comes from an office manager, or directly from the person who's doing the hiring.

WHAT IS THE TEMPORARY AGENCY TOLD ABOUT THE JOB?

A temporary agency is given much less information about a job than an employment agency. Since most jobs are short-term, the company is not as concerned with matching up the right personality to the right job. The temporary counselor is usually told only basic information: the hours of the job, the location of the company, the floor, what you will be doing on that job, and how long the job is expected to last. She may also be told the lunch policy. (Temporary workers only get paid for the hours they work, so if you work nine to five with one hour for lunch, it's a seven-hour day. If you take a half-hour lunch, it's a seven-and-a-half-hour day. Some companies require that you take an hour, some a half hour.)

HOW LONG DO TEMP JOBS USUALLY LAST?

Jobs assignments range anywhere from a day on up— there are some people that have been in temporary positions with the same company for over a year. Due to the recession, many companies are now opting for what is called a "payroll transfer." The client will call the temporary agency and say "I have interviewed someone I would really like to hire as a full-time employee. However, it's not in our permanent budget to pay for benefits, or for vacation and holiday time. So I'm going to send her over to you." The temporary agency becomes the employer and takes on all costs for the employee. The company is then responsible for paying only the agency's fees. It's cost-effective for the company to use temps; however, it's not necessarily to your benefit to accept such an offer. Most temporary agencies will pay your salary, but can offer you only limited benefits, if any.

HOW ARE TEMPORARY-AGENCY JOBS ADVERTISED?

Temporary agencies seldom run an ad for a particular job. Instead they usually run ads for the particular skills they may need that week (such as knowledge of a particular software program). Legally, the ads must state that they are for a temporary agency. Ads tend to be very general, including such information as, "long- and short-term assignments available, day hours, competitive rates, immediate hire. Come in Monday."

The ads can often be found in several different places within the want-ads section of the newspaper. If the temporary agency has word-processing work available in a publishing firm, for example, it usually advertises under "publishing," under "temporary work," and under "word processing."

DO I HAVE TO CALL FOR AN APPOINTMENT?

Unlike employment agencies, most temporary agencies don't see people by appointment. If you call in response to an ad, you're usually told to come in and fill out an application. It's not even necessary to call in advance. If you do phone first, and say you're calling about a specific secretarial job, for example, the agency might ask, "How fast do you type?" If you don't meet the requirements of that specific job, you'll be told to come in and fill out an application for other available positions.

WHAT IS ON THE APPLICATION FORM?

An application for temporary work can be very detailed. It includes all the basic information (name, address, phone number), but it also asks for detailed scheduling data. The agency needs to know when and how often you'll be available so they know what type of jobs to send you out on.

If you are on summer vacation from school, for example, you may be able to take a two-month-long assignment. If you're available only one or two days a week, you'll be sent on only short-term assignments. You'll be asked if your schedule allows you to work overtime if necessary.

You may be asked if you're interested in a specific kind of industry. If you say that you're particularly interested in working for advertising firms, the agency may ask if you're willing to work elsewhere if they can't find you advertising work. The application will ask you for information about your skills and experience.

IS THERE ANYTHING I NEED TO BRING WITH ME TO THE INTERVIEW?

You should always bring your résumé. And because the temporary agency will be your employer, it is required to see two forms of identification (passport, driver's license, birth certificate) in order to determine that you are legally working in this country.

WHAT HAPPENS AFTER I FILL OUT AN APPLICATION?

You will then be tested to determine your skill levels. Depending on what type of jobs you're looking for, you'll be tested on spelling, simple math, typing, and/or word processing.

After your tests are scored, you will be assigned to a counselor. Usually, you work with this counselor as long as you stay with this agency. After she has reviewed your application, the counselor will interview you.

WHAT KINDS OF QUESTIONS WILL A COUNSELOR ASK ME?

You may be asked questions such as:

- *Why you are looking for temporary work?* The counselor is not trying to pry into your private life, she's trying to determine what your availability will be. If she knows that you are temping while looking for a permanent position, she may not want to send you out on a long-term spot. If she knows that you're in school and are only available on certain days, she'll know to place you only on those days.
- *Is there anything you would not like or would refuse to do?* Some applicants are very specific about what they will and will not do on the job. You may not want to run personal errands, or to make coffee for the boss. You may not want to work in a smoking environment. You may have restrictions about where you will work—if you need to work only within a limited commuting distance, for instance, let the counselor know.

  You may have a conflict about going to a certain

type of company. For example, if you have worked in publishing as an editor, and are now seeking word-processing temporary work, you may not want to go to publishing firms where you may run into people you know. Whatever your reason for not wanting to go to a particular place or do a particular kind of work, let the counselor know during this interview. The more specific you are, the better chance the agency has of placing you correctly.

• *What hourly rate are you looking for?* Counselors usually ask this because they want to know how much (or how little) you'll accept, and if you have a realistic idea of how much you'll be making. If at all possible, ask people you know with similar skills who are working temp what they make. That way you'll be able to tell if this agency is offering competitive rates. How much you make an hour differs from city to city and from agency to agency. It also depends on the individual company for whom you are working at any given time. So you may make nine dollars an hour one day and eleven the next for the same type of work.

HOW DO I GET PAID?

Most temporary agencies work on a time-sheet basis. For each job you go on, you fill in the days and hours worked, subtract your lunch hours, and fill in the totals. The time sheet must be signed by the supervisor at the job. Then you either call or send in your hours to the agency. They may mail your paycheck, or you may be able to come to the office to pick it up. Since the agency is your employer, they take out all necessary taxes.

SHOP FOR AN AGENCY YOU LIKE

SHOULD I REGISTER WITH MORE THAN ONE AGENCY?

Many people register with more than one agency in order to increase the number of job possibilities. As with employment agencies, shop around until you find one, or more than one, with which you feel comfortable. Ask yourself, "What makes this agency any different than any other agency?"

SECRET STRATEGY NUMBER 18:
Since most temporary agencies provide the same services, work only for the one(s) that you like and trust.

IS THERE A GOOD TIME TO APPLY FOR TEMPORARY WORK?

While you can apply at any time, one of the best times is in the fall. Over the summer, agencies are usually flooded with college students looking for work. When they go back to school, agencies are in need of applicants to take their place.

Surprisingly, agencies claim that they never have enough applicants. With the unemployment rate so high, they expect to have about twenty applicants for each job opening, but that is not usually the case. However, there may not be work for you immediately. Although an agency may have an abundance of jobs, the jobs may not be right for your skill level. If you're looking for receptionist work, and all they have are word-processing positions, you may have to wait until more jobs come in.

QUESTIONING THE COUNSELOR

Bring a list of questions with you. The counselor may not have a lot of information about each particular job on which she will send you, but you can ask her about how the agency works. Here are some of the questions you should be asking your counselor. The first question you should ask is:

- •*Do you charge a fee?* A temporary agency should not be charging you a fee. They are paid by the companies that hire them. If you are asked to pay a placement fee, go elsewhere.

When you are given a job assignment, you should ask:

- •*Who will I be working for?* Find out the person's name, his or her title, and any information you can get about his or her personality.
- •*What will I be doing when I get there?* Ask for specifics. If a counselor tells you you'll be going on a secretarial spot at a particular company, what does that mean? Will you be typing? Filing? Word processing? Will you be expected to get lunch, make coffee, etc.? The better prepared you are, the better job you'll do when you get there.
- •*What can I expect when I get to the job?* It can be unnerving to go to work at a different company every day. You never know what you'll be walking into. You might work at a Fortune 500 company one day and at a mom-and-pop organization the next. That's why it's important to ask what kind of company it is, and how many people are on staff. Ask the counselor what she knows about how you'll be treated. Some companies will take you around, introduce

you to everyone, and make you feel at home. Others will sit you down at a desk, give you your work, and leave you alone.

- *What is the hourly rate for this job?* You cannot assume you will get the same rate for every job, even though you are doing similar work. It depends on how much each company is paying the temp agency. If the hourly rate is less than you feel is acceptable, tell the counselor you would prefer to wait until something higher comes along (if you can afford to do that).

- *Can I ever get a raise on my hourly rate?* You always negotiate money matters with the temporary agency (as opposed to negotiating with the company for which you're working). If you've been working on a job for several weeks (or even months), and you feel you deserve a raise, talk to your counselor. If she feels a raise is possible, she will negotiate with the company.

Sometimes, you may find that a job has been described to you incorrectly. Usually that's because it has been described to the agency incorrectly. For example, a company may call the temporary agency and say they need someone for light typing and filing. If you get to the job and they ask you to do heavy word processing, you should call your counselor and apprise her of the situation. If the company is willing to teach you word processing, you may stay at the same rate and get the benefit of learning a new skill. But if you already know word processing, and the company wants to take advantage of your skills, you are entitled to a higher rate. If you have any questions about what you are entitled to, call the agency.

*   *   *

Temporary work can be very useful. It's often a good opportunity to shine on a job. Many people are offered full-time positions once they have proven themselves working on a temporary basis. If you are thinking of working temp, be a smart shopper. Look for an agency with a professional staff and a good reputation.

If you are in the market for an executive position, you may want to consider a headhunter or executive search firm. The next chapter will provide you with the basics you need to make the best possible use of this type of agency.

SECTION 13

SMART QUESTIONS TO ASK ABOUT THE EXECUTIVE-SEARCH-FIRM (HEADHUNTER) INTERVIEW

PICTURE THIS:

You are sitting in your office staring at the computer screen, going over some spread-sheet figures. The phone rings and you pick it up, your mind still on the company's disappointing third quarter. A voice on the other end says, "Ms. Harper? This is Arnold Fine. I'm with the executive search firm of Smith and Jones, and we have a vice-president of finance position to fill at a Fortune 500 organization. I wonder if you have a few minutes to speak with me?"

Talk about out of the blue! It might be that you've been thinking about leaving your present position—or perhaps it's never entered your mind. Suddenly an opportunity opens up before you. How do you respond?

A good way to respond is cautiously, but with interest.

The executive search firm, or headhunter as it's more commonly called, is the only type of placement service where the interviewer generally calls you first. In years past, this used to be the only way to get connected with headhunters. Once again, the downturned economy has changed business procedures; it is now perfectly accept-able (and advisable) to send them your résumé.

There is a gentleman named Marvin Berenblum at the firm of Heidrick & Struggles, in Greenwich, Connecticut, whose years of experience and broad knowledge of the placement business were extremely helpful in working on this section.

HOW AN EXECUTIVE SEARCH FIRM WORKS

WHAT TYPES OF JOBS DO EXECUTIVE SEARCH FIRMS USUALLY HANDLE?

Headhunters usually work on executive-level positions paying anywhere from $50,000 on up. They are hired, and paid by, companies looking to fill a particular position. If a headhunter calls you, it means that you are a close match to a company's specifications.

HOW ARE HEADHUNTERS PAID?

Headhunters are paid in two ways. One is that they are hired on a retainer by a company—which means that they get paid for doing the search, and will get their money whether they find someone to fill the position or not. The other method is that they get paid on contingency—which means they get paid only if they find someone for the job. It is to your advantage to work with a headhunter who is on retainer. He can afford to work harder to make a perfect match for his client.

WHAT ARE THE CHANCES OF GETTING A JOB THROUGH AN EXECUTIVE SEARCH FIRM?

The odds of getting a job through a search firm are not the best. A headhunter may contact one hundred possible candidates for one job. Out of those one hundred, he will usually discuss fifteen or twenty with the client. The headhunter may then interview ten or twelve out of that group, and pass five or six on to the client. Two or three of those candidates may make it to a second round of interviews with the client.

IS IT A GOOD IDEA TO SEND MY RÉSUMÉ TO AN EXECUTIVE SEARCH FIRM?

It can't hurt. But if you do, he'll probably put your name in his files. Don't expect to hear from him anytime soon, as the odds are slim he will be looking for someone with your background just at the moment he receives your resume.

HOW TO GET A HEADHUNTER TO CALL

Headhunters receive dozens of résumés every week. On paper, everyone tends to look the same. Headhunters are looking for the "stars" of the industry, the people who stand out from the crowd. They get some of their best leads from networking. So if they ask someone "Do you know of anyone who might be perfect for this job?" you want your name to come to mind.

How do you get your name out there? By being your own public-relations consultant.

SECRET STRATEGY NUMBER 19:
If you want headhunters to call, make your name
a household—or industry-wide—word.
High visibility is the key.

HOW CAN I BECOME A VISIBLE PRESENCE WITHIN MY INDUSTRY?

Here are eight ways to go about it:

1. *Get your name in print:* Write articles about your particular area of expertise and send them to your company newsletter, business magazines, trade publications, alumni magazines, and the business section of your local newspaper.

2. *Write letters to the editor:* One good way to break into print is to respond to articles you've read. If you strongly agree or disagree with a position taken, let the editor know. Back up your opinion with facts and figures. Include the name of your company or industry as a positive example to illustrate your point.

3. *Try radio and TV:* Although it may be difficult to break into these arenas, you can start with local programming. Many local and cable programs are on the lookout for business-oriented talk-show guests and expert panelists for news or public-service

programs. Contact the producers of particular shows that interest you, or the news director for the station.

4. *Be visible in your community:* Volunteer for activities, serve on committees, speak before local business organizations.

5. *Run for office in your trade association:* Even if you don't win, your name (and accomplishments) will become well known.

6. *Become a board member:* Serve on the board(s) of worthy organizations or institutions, such as hospitals or community fund-raising groups.

7. *Take advantage of in-house PR facilities:* Make sure the in-house PR department knows all about your activities and achievements—but be sure to share credit when it needs to be shared.

8. *Do your own PR:* If your company doesn't have an in-house department, do your own promotion. Send announcements of job changes, promotions, awards, and presentations to newspapers, trade publications, alumni magazines, etc.

High visibility—keeping your name in front of the public eye—will help you get ahead faster. It will also make it easier for a headhunter to put your name at the top of his list.

WHAT TO DO WHEN A HEADHUNTER CALLS—OR WRITES

HOW DOES A HEADHUNTER CONTACT SOMEONE IN WHOM HE IS INTERESTED?

Most headhunters use the phone. However, you may

receive a letter giving you sketchy details of an available position, and asking if you'd care to respond. The letter might even say, "We'd be grateful if you can suggest anyone who might be interested in this position." If you do know anyone, including yourself, respond.

WHAT SHOULD I KNOW ABOUT THE FIRM BEFORE I RESPOND?

Before you make any response, or before you send your résumé to any firm, do some research on your own. Go to the library and see if you can find information in a directory of executive search firms. Call the Better Business Bureau. Ask your friends and colleagues if anyone has heard of, or has had any dealings with this firm. Call trade or professional associations in your industry and find out if they have had any dealing with, or have any information about this firm.

CAN I GET INFORMATION DIRECTLY FROM THE FIRM?

You can call the firm directly without revealing your name and ask:

- *If I send a résumé or reply, will my response be kept confidential? Will you send my résumé out to clients without my knowledge?* If you are currently working, you may not want it spread all over town that you're looking for a new job. Even if you're unemployed, you want control over your job search. You don't want your résumé sent out indiscriminately. A reputable firm will discuss any possibilities with you before they proceed to send your résumé to the client.

- *What level of responsibility does this firm cover? What salary range?* If you're a corporate vice-president making $200,000 a year, you don't want to get involved with a firm that works only with middle management. Conversely, if you're looking for a $50,000-a-year range, you don't want to waste your résumé sending it to a firm that deals only with high-level executives who make over $100,000.
- *Does this firm specialize in a particular industry?* If you can find a headhunter who specializes in your industry, this is the direction to take. This firm will know the ins and outs of your industry, and will probably be known by the companies seeking placement services.
- *Is there a particular person at this firm who specializes in a specific industry?* A larger search firm may handle several different industries, but have one person to handle each particular industry. You want to speak to, or write to, that person.

WHAT SHOULD I DO IF A HEADHUNTER CALLS ME "OUT OF THE BLUE"?

Keep your initial conversation brief and to the point. You might say, "I'm interested in speaking with you, but it is not convenient at the moment." Then do your research and call him back if you're still interested.

Headhunters will usually contact you at your office. If you're uncomfortable speaking there, you might say, "I can't talk right now. Would it be possible for me to call you at home this evening?" Do not give out your home number. A reputable headhunter understands the office situation and won't mind being called at home.

THE INITIAL CONVERSATION

If you do take the initial call, or call back to express your interest, expect this to be a fairly short conversation. At this point, the headhunter knows more about you than you know about him or the job. As with the other placement services discussed, you should interview the interviewer.

Here are some questions you should ask the headhunter:

- *How long have you been in this business? How long have you been with this firm?* You want to know if you're dealing with an experienced headhunter or with someone new to the business. You want to try to work with a headhunter who has been with this firm for at least a year. If the headhunter has been there awhile, she's probably very familiar with the needs of her clients, and what types of applicants match their needs best.
- *Do you specialize in this industry? How much experience do you have working with this industry?* Obviously, if they specialize in the industry, and/or have a history of dealing with your field, they're more knowledgeable about what it takes to succeed in this industry, and what individual companies are looking for.
- *Are you on retainer with this client, or on a contingency basis?* If she is on contingency, she may not be as careful about making a perfect match.
- *Have you worked with this client before?* The better the headhunter knows the client, the more he can tell you about the job. Also, repeat business shows that the client has confidence in this particular headhunter.

WHAT DO I NEED TO KNOW ABOUT THE JOB BEING OFFERED?

At this point, the headhunter will probably not reveal the name of the company, or go into great detail about the job. If you express interest, he may invite you to come for an in-person interview. But you do want to get preliminary information so you can decide just how interested you are. Ask:

- *What are the major responsibilities of the job?* You want to know if this is a job that would interest you and keep you challenged.
- *What is the corporate culture like?* If you're used to and enjoy working in a casual, informal atmosphere, and the job is in an old-fashioned, conservative firm, you may not be happy there. You should know this up front so you'll know whether or not to keep the conversation going.
- *Is it a large or a small company?* If you have a personal preference for one or the other, this information could influence your decision.
- *Will it require relocation?* Some search firms interview candidates from all over the country. The headhunter could be calling you for a job hundreds of miles from where you're presently located. What kinds of problems would moving entail? Are you willing to consider them, or do you have other obligations that keep you where you are?
- *Why is this position open?* You want to know if this is a newly created position, if the job is open because the previous employee was promoted or left for personal reasons, or if the previous employee was fired. If he or she was fired, try to find out why.

• *What is the compensation?* You are not making a bottom-line negotiation here, you're asking for a ballpark figure. The headhunter may give you a firm figure, or he may give you a range.

WHAT HAPPENS AFTER OUR INITIAL CONVERSATION?

At the end of this conversation you'll be expected to let the headhunter know whether or not you're interested in the job. Even if you are not interested in this particular job, encourage the headhunter to keep you in mind for future possibilities.

If you say yes, you may be immediately invited to come in for an interview, or the headhunter may have to consult with his client first.

THE IN-PERSON INTERVIEW

You may be asked to come into the headhunter's office for a formal interview. Some headhunters prefer to meet informally, over breakfast or lunch. Wherever you meet, you must prepare thoroughly.

HOW DOES AN INTERVIEW WITH A HEADHUNTER DIFFER FROM AN INTERVIEW WITH AN EMPLOYER?

This interview may not differ greatly from an interview you might have directly with the potential employer; however, the headhunter is probably more skilled at interviewing. Headhunters, like bosses, are looking for more than just the required skills. They're also looking at the success factors (see Section 3).

WHAT KINDS OF QUESTIONS MIGHT I BE ASKED DURING AN INTERVIEW?

Here are a few examples of questions you might be asked (for more questions you might be asked by either the headhunter or a potential employer, see Section 17):

- What kind of student were you?
- Did you work during school? If so, where and why?
- What kind of person would be your ideal boss?
- How would you describe your ideal job?
- What are the responsibilities of your current job?
- Have you ever made a large mistake in your career, and if so, how did you fix it?
- Are you a risk-taker?
- What do you think makes a successful executive?
- What excites you about your current job or about your industry?
- What are the most positive attributes of your current job? The most negative?

QUESTIONING THE HEADHUNTER

Of course, you want to get as much information as you can about the job. Don't be afraid to ask questions. Often, you can get a more objective answer about a job or a company from a headhunter than you would from the boss herself.

Here are some of the questions you should be asking:

- How long has this position been available?
- How many other applicants have you interviewed for this position?

- •Why have none of the other applicants gotten the job yet?
- •To whom would I report in this position?
- •What is the turnover rate in this department?
- •What are the company's overall objectives?
- •What exactly are the company's products or services?
- •How is this company ranked within the industry?
- •What personal characteristics make for a successful executive in this company?
- •What are the growth opportunities in this company?

One of the best ways you can impress a headhunter is by asking intelligent questions. You should also give truthful, thoughtful answers to questions you are asked. Interviewers don't want to hear pat answers. They want to learn about you.

Whatever happens, remain on good terms with the headhunter. Send her a thank-you note whether or not you get a job offer. Let her know that she can call again for jobs she thinks might interest you, or as a source for supplying her potential candidates.

The last three chapters have concentrated on independent placement services. Read on for information about the "dreaded," but often unavoidable, in-house personnel interview.

SMART QUESTIONS TO ASK ABOUT THE PERSONNEL-DEPARTMENT INTERVIEW

There are some times in life when you simply cannot avoid doing something you'd rather not do—and going through personnel to get a job is often one of them. Though the best way to get a job is to go directly to the person for whom you want to work, this is not always possible. Sometimes, you *have* to go through personnel.

Personnel's job is to weed people out. The personnel interviewer does not want to send an obviously unqualified candidate to the manager who is looking for an employee. She is going to look at your résumé and your job qualifications to try to find the perfect fit, and any deviations are going to make a negative impression.

However, personnel executives are not out to get

you—they just have a job to do. Like employment agents and headhunters, they're looking to make an ideal match between applicant and employer. If you're lucky enough to deal with a good personnel exec—and if you meet the exact job requirements she has been given—you should have no problem getting to the next round of interviews.

Two excellent personnel executives were very forthcoming and helpful for this section: Gloria Kessler, Personnel Director, Corporate Administration for Condé Nast Publications, and Patricia O'Leary, Personnel Manager at FCIA Management Company.

HOW THE PERSONNEL DEPARTMENT WORKS

DOES EVERYONE WHO APPLIES FOR A JOB HAVE TO GO THROUGH PERSONNEL?

Every company has its own hiring policies. Many companies insist that everyone below the "rank" of vice-president go through personnel—even the boss's nephew or the CEO's brother-in-law. Other companies are not as strict. If you come to the organization and get an interview with the potential boss through your own efforts, you may only be sent to personnel to fill out the necessary forms for payroll, health-care benefits, etc.

HOW DO I GET IN TO SEE PERSONNEL?

There are many routes to the personnel office. One is through the classified ads; jobs that are advertised in the newspaper usually refer you to someone in personnel.

You might also come to the personnel department through a referral or recommendation of someone in the company. Some personnel departments find job applicants through employment agencies, and some go through their files for people who have previously applied for jobs, but were not hired at the time.

Sometimes, even if you call or write directly to a potential employer, she will say, "I'd like to talk to you, but company policy says that everyone has to go through personnel." If that happens, say "I appreciate your interest. Can I use your name when I talk to personnel?" That way, you can call personnel and tell them that Sally Jones is considering hiring you, and recommended you call their office.

Another option is to make a "cold call"—just pick up the phone and call personnel directly, ask if there are any openings in your particular field, and if it's possible to get an interview.

IF THE COMPANY PLACES AN AD IN THE PAPER, TO WHOM ARE THE RESPONSES SENT?

Only in a very small company will the responses go directly to the potential boss. In most larger companies, responses go to personnel.

HOW MANY RESPONSES ARE TYPICALLY RECEIVED FOR ONE OPENING?

This really depends on the type of job advertised. Higher-level jobs receive fewer responses. An ad for a position such as production supervisor might get forty responses; an ad for a secretary might get two hundred.

HOW IMPORTANT IS THE APPEARANCE OF THE RÉSUMÉ?

It's certainly a factor. If a resume looks like it's been reprinted for the thirty-seventh time, if it contains typos, if it's got lipstick smudges on the corner or chocolate stains over your name, you won't be called in for an interview. Flashy résumés (on colored paper or glossy stock, for example) may get someone's attention—but if the content isn't what personnel is looking for, you won't be considered.

OUT OF THOSE TWO-HUNDRED RÉSUMÉS, HOW MANY PEOPLE GET CALLED FOR INTERVIEWS?

Unfortunately, the odds are against you in this situation. Usually very few people get called—perhaps six to twelve. Personnel executives often complain that too many people don't really read the ads. It seems to them that people are simply sending out mass mailings of résumés whether or not they are particularly qualified for the job.

If you are changing careers, or even changing fields within a specific industry, answering this kind of ad will probably do you no good. Once again, personnel is looking for a perfect fit; with so many applicants to choose from, they will call only those who are closely matched.

WHO CALLS THE SELECTED APPLICANTS?

If you've been selected to come in for an interview, the personnel executive, or an assistant, will call you. You will be prescreened at this time. The conversation will probably be brief, but the interviewer will try to get an idea of your personality, your professionalism, and your interest in the job.

A word of advice: Be very careful about the outgoing message on your answering machine. A barrage of jokes or several minutes of funky music may be fine for your friends and family—but a potential employer may not be amused. If you're seriously job hunting, your message should be brief and straightforward.

WHAT WILL THE PERSONNEL INTERVIEW BE LIKE?

There are as many different types of personnel interviews as their are personnel executives. An interview can be very formal, or it can seem like a fireside chat. In fact, some interviewers prefer an informal atmosphere. They feel that if they can get you to relax, you will be much more candid in your replies; if you think of the interviewer as a friend as opposed to a foe, you won't be so focused on trying to impress her.

The interviewer is not trying to trick you; she's trying to find out what you're really like. She is trying to discover the "chemistry" aspect—how well you will mix with the rest of the team. It's up to you to remain professional, and to remember your purpose at all times. It is perfectly okay to laugh and joke with the interviewer (if this is the tone that has been set) as long as you remain in control.

WHAT KINDS OF QUESTIONS WILL BE ASKED?

Once again, there is no way to tell in advance what questions you'll be asked. But most interviewers ask the typical questions about your education, and why you chose the particular classes and/or school you attended. They'll ask you about your work experience, about what you did on the job, and why you left. But because personnel executives are trained in the art of interviewing, many strive to avoid standard questions that they know people are prepared to answer, and ask more unorthodox questions. Here are some examples:

- What are the skills and abilities you have that you would most like to develop?
- What annoys you on a job?
- What's the most difficult political situation you ever faced on the job?
- Who was the most difficult person you ever worked for and how did you cope?
- What was your most memorable day at work?
- Why do you want to work for this company?

WHAT QUALITIES, OTHER THAN REQUIRED SKILLS, ARE IMPORTANT TO INTERVIEWERS?

Like all other interviewers, personnel executives are looking for the success factors discussed in Section 3. Often, a sense of humor is also an important factor. If you can demonstrate a sense of humor despite the tension of an interview, you can probably handle the pressures of the job.

When you're at a personnel interview, sell yourself by stressing the success factors. Let the interviewer know that you're adaptable, for example—that you can easily adjust to a new boss's style and demands. Let her know that you're committed to doing your best at all times. Be articulate and demonstrate your communications skills. By emphasizing your success factors, you stand a much better chance of being recommended for a second interview.

WHAT REALLY IMPRESSES INTERVIEWERS?

Thoughtful responses. Interviewers are looking for people who think about their answers and do not just spout replies they think the interviewer wants to hear. They're looking for people who ask thoughtful and intelligent questions as well; people who are genuinely interested in the way the organization works and in the overall management style.

WHAT TURNS AN INTERVIEWER OFF?

People who lie. We all want to show ourselves in the best possible light, and you should know how to emphasize your strengths and play down your weaknesses. But you must be honest at the same time. If you are caught in a lie or an exaggeration, you will not be considered for the job.

Interviewers are turned off by people who look like they'd rather not be at the interview. No matter how uncomfortable you are at an interview, don't let the interviewer see it. Discomfort can easily be perceived as disinterest.

Personnel executives see an interview as a good indication of how you will do under pressure. They dislike people who get defensive during an interview, people who don't answer their questions, and people who talk too much without really saying anything.

FIRST THINGS FIRST

Preparation for an interview with personnel should be just as thorough as that for any other interview. In fact, you may even need more preparation, since these people are expert interviewers.

WHAT IS THE BEST WAY TO PREPARE FOR AN INTERVIEW?

You should be well versed on the basic questions that all interviewers are going to ask. You should be able to talk about your previous employment, including what you did on a daily basis, how you responded to crises, your major accomplishments, and how you handled your relationships with supervisors, subordinates, and peers.

Here are some hints about steps to take before your interview takes place:

- *Find out about the corporate culture.* Is this a conservative firm or a casual one? How do people dress? If you don't know the company, perhaps you can drop by the office one day first thing in the morning or at lunchtime and watch people coming in and out. Notice how they are dressed and what kind of attaché cases they carry. If you can't get to the office before your interview, call the receptionist. Be honest with her. Tell her you have an interview coming up and ask, "If you have a minute, could you give me an idea of what your company is like? What do people wear every day?" If she's busy, ask her when you can call back. Personnel will be very concerned with whether or not you fit into the company "team," so you want to be sure to be dressed appropriately.
- *Get to know as much as possible about the company.* Do your homework. Go to the library. Call the company and ask the receptionist to send you an annual report. Try to talk with people who work there, or have worked there in the past. Personnel executives

are impressed by people who ask intelligent questions about the company based on prior knowledge. They are immediately turned off by someone who asks, "Exactly what does this company do?"

- *Practice your interviewing techniques.* Use your friends and family to help you out. In any interview situation, be yourself and answer questions as honestly as you can. Know what your strengths are, and how best to sell yourself, but don't think you can just reel off answers that you practiced at home.

WHAT HAPPENS IF I GO TO AN INTERVIEW WITH PERSONNEL AND I'M NOT RIGHT FOR THE PARTICULAR JOB? IS THAT THE LAST I'LL EVER HEAR FROM THEM?

Not if you play your cards right. When you go for an interview with a potential employer, especially in large companies, you are usually interviewing for one specific job. If you don't get that job, the story ends right there. The advantage of interviewing with personnel is that although you may go there for a specific job, personnel deals with the entire company and may know of other positions for which you may be better suited.

IS IT HARDER TO "SELL" MYSELF TO A PERSONNEL EXECUTIVE OR DIRECTLY TO A POTENTIAL EMPLOYER?

You may have more of a problem with a personnel executive if you don't exactly fit the requirements of the particular job. When you're talking directly to an employer, you can use your own questioning and listening skills to find out his or her wants and needs, and sell yourself accordingly. It's more difficult to do that when you are speaking to a personnel executive who may have a slightly different agenda.

Personnel executives are experts at their jobs. They have studied the art and skill of interviewing (as opposed to most bosses, who may be good at their jobs but don't know much about interviewing). As long as you understand the purpose of this interview, which is to build rapport and make connections, you can learn how to get personnel on your side, how to sell your strengths, and how to tell the interviewer what she needs to hear in order to pass you on to the real decision maker.

SECRET STRATEGY NUMBER 20:
Use your interviews with personnel executives
to create an impression, build rapport, and
take advantage of their many connections.

DOES THAT MEAN I SHOULD TRY TO MAKE FRIENDS WITH THE PERSONNEL EXECUTIVE?

You don't need to become the personnel executive's best friend. But do try to establish—and keep up—a rapport. As soon as the interview ends, send a thank-you note. Don't wait to hear whether or not you got sent on to the boss—thank her for her time and an interesting interview.

WHAT SHOULD I DO IF I GET SENT ON FOR A SECOND INTERVIEW, BUT DON'T GET THE JOB?

Thank the personnel executive anyway. You may want to call her and ask if she knows about other jobs within that company. If there are no other openings at present, ask her to keep you in mind for future jobs. If it's a company you'd really like to work for, send her little notes or call occasionally to remind her of who you are, and that you are still looking. You might also want to ask if she knows personnel executives in other companies, and could put in a good word for you.

WHAT SHOULD I DO IF I DO GET THE JOB?

If you do get the job, make sure you thank her again. Keep in touch, even if you have no official reason. You never know when you may want to use her services again. She might move to another company, and you may at some point apply for a job there. Or you may have friends or colleagues that you want to recommend for jobs. Since these times are so uncertain, it never hurts to keep closely connected with personnel.

SUPPOSE I'M ONE OF THE TWO OR THREE CANDIDATES THE PERSONNEL INTERVIEWER DECIDES SHE LIKES. WHAT WILL SHE TELL THE POTENTIAL BOSS ABOUT ME?

The personnel executive will probably fill the boss in on any factual information that is not on your résumé—for instance, why you left your last job. Some will also voice any hesitations they may have. Others prefer not to talk about any reservations until after the interview, because they don't want to influence the boss's judgment.

AFTER THAT INTERVIEW, WILL THE BOSS DISCUSS MY APPLICATION WITH THE PERSONNEL EXECUTIVE?

It depends on the individual boss, and on company policy. But many bosses do like to discuss candidates with personnel to compare notes and swap impressions before they make a final hiring decision.

HOW AND WHEN IS MONEY DISCUSSED?

This varies from company to company and with the type of job involved. For some higher-level positions, money will be discussed with the potential boss. For most entry and nonsupervisory-level positions, money issues are handled by the personnel executive.

Often, when you're first asked to send in a résumé, you will also be asked to send your salary requirements. If you don't include that information, you may be asked the question in the prescreening phone call. If you're forced to discuss money up front, try to get the personnel executive to be the first to mention an actual figure. They will usually give you a range, such as "We're paying between $35,000 and $37,000." Once you've actually been offered the job, personnel will often give you the final salary offer (plus benefits, if any).

YOUR TURN: WHAT YOU SHOULD BE ASKING

Interviewers are always impressed by people who ask questions. The questions you ask can often make the difference in getting hired or getting passed over. One personnel executive I know told me about a young woman who recently came into her office for an interview. She had a very thick accent, so thick that it was at times difficult to understand her. But she had researched the company thoroughly, and came in with about a dozen very intelligent questions pertaining to the company. She got the job.

WHAT KINDS OF QUESTIONS SHOULD I BE ASKING?

Don't be a pest with your questions, and don't try to embarrass the interviewer by trying to prove you know more than she does. However, do ask questions. Here are some sample questions you might ask at a personnel interview:

- What is the management style in this organization?
- How will I be evaluated? How is my work going to be judged?
- What are the main responsibilities of this job?
- How would you describe this boss's management style?
- What type of person tends to succeed working for this person?
- Where can this job lead?
- Why did the last person leave this position?
- What kind of turnover do you have?

A FEW WORDS OF ADVICE

I'VE BEEN LOOKING FOR WORK FOR SEVERAL MONTHS NOW. WILL BEING OUT OF WORK FOR THIS LENGTH OF TIME HURT MY CHANCES WITH THE PERSONNEL EXECUTIVE?

Often your attitude is more important than the fact that you've been out of work for a while. This advice comes from Patricia O'Leary of FCIA Management Company: "If you've been out on the market for a while—and I sympathize with anybody who has been—do not get that hangdog 'please hire me' look. Recently I interviewed two women for word-processing jobs. They were both older women; they had both worked for other companies for about twenty-five years. Both of them had gotten laid off from their previous jobs. They came in one day apart. One woman sat there practically in tears. I felt very badly for her, but she appeared so personally hurt, she never mentioned that five hundred other people were laid off with her. She came in with the attitude, 'I know I'm not going to get this job.' The next day the other woman came in and she said, 'Yes, I got laid off. It's part of life in the big city. So here I am, I need a new job, and I'm ready to go back to work.' I hired her."

WHAT'S THE BEST WAY TO DEAL WITH REJECTION?

You cannot take a rejection personally. There are too many factors that go into a hiring decision. It's all right to analyze an interview when it's over and ask yourself what you can do to improve for the next time, but you can't try to guess why you weren't hired. Maybe the company decided not to hire anyone. Maybe they decided to hire their client's son, maybe they changed the job description. Don't waste your time beating yourself up for something that may not have had anything to do with you.

Now that we've discussed the basics of interviewing and the preliminary interviews you may run into, it's time to move on to the ultimate interview. Your goal in all these interviews is to come face-to-face with the potential employer. The next six sections will give you the tips, tools, and techniques you need to master the art of interviewing the employer.

PART III:

TIPS, TOOLS, AND TECHNIQUES: MASTERING THE ART OF INTERVIEWING THE EMPLOYER

SMART QUESTIONS TO ASK ABOUT THE "HIDDEN" INTERVIEWS: WHEN TO WRITE, WHEN TO PHONE, AND WHEN *NOT* TO SEND A RÉSUMÉ

If only 10 percent of all interviews are generated from classified ads, and perhaps 10 percent come from the rest of the sources discussed in the previous sections, how can you tap into the other 80 percent of interview opportunities? These are the hidden interviews, the ones that are not advertised in the paper, posted on bulletin boards, or exposed at job fairs. These are the interviews that you discover by putting on your job detective gear and using the tools of the trade.

What are those tools? Very simply, they are the introductory letter, the phone call, and sometimes—but not always—the résumé.

* * *

THE INTRODUCTORY LETTER

You already know a lot about this vital technique for getting interviews. You used it to get information interviews, and to get the jump on the competition when responding to an advertised position. But if you wait for a position to be advertised, it's probably already too late.

You want to get to employers before they advertise the jobs—sometimes even before a job has become available. The best way to accomplish this goal is to send an introductory letter.

WHAT IS THE PURPOSE OF MY INTRODUCTORY LETTER?

The specific objective of this letter is to arouse a prospective employer's interest enough so that when you call, he or she will be anxious to speak with you. Its purpose is to pique the employer's interest—to convince this person that you are someone worth seeing. You do this by sending the right letter to the right person.

SECRET STRATEGY NUMBER 21:
Sending the right letter to the right person gives you a jump on the competition and makes you a likely interview candidate.

HOW DO I KNOW WHO THE "RIGHT PERSON" IS?

Your list of possible employers comes out of the research you did in Section 2. You determine what kinds of companies you'd like to work for, which companies meet your criteria, and who at those companies has the hiring authority. (As we discussed earlier, introductory letters, with slight variations, are also the most effective method for getting information and networking interviews.)

Your research will result in what is known as a *targeted list*—it's not just a random sampling of names, but a carefully considered group of people who all have an interest in the product or service you have to "sell."

NOW THAT I HAVE MY TARGETED LIST, WHAT SHOULD MY LETTER CONTAIN?

An effective letter contains an interest-getter; the answer to the employer's question "What's in it for me?" The offer to your employer is that you will do for him what you have done for others: "Make me a part of your team and I'll solve your distribution problem." "Make me a part of your team and I'll help increase productivity." One or two of your most relevant accomplishments, presented in terms of clearly applicable benefit to the reader, will often make a prospective employer grant you an interview even if there is no immediate opening.

WHAT DOES AN EMPLOYER LOOK FOR WHEN SHE GETS SUCH A LETTER?

Of course, she looks for relevant content. However, the first thing she'll notice is the appearance of your letter. It must be perfectly and professionally typed. No matter how talented you are, or how impressive your past accomplishments, no employer will take a second look at a letter that does not reflect quality and concern for detail. There must be no typos or grammatical errors, and no ripped, torn, stained, or mutilated pages.

The most successful letters include these five important points:

1. *Get the name right!* This is a *personalized* letter, so be sure you have the right person. Letters addressed "Dear Division President" are unacceptable. You want to reach the decision maker, the person who has direct responsibility for hiring you—or the person who has the most useful information for you, or the most valuable contacts. Call the company and make sure you have the correct spelling and title.

2. *Make the reader feel special.* Open with a statement that lets the reader know this is not a mass mailing. Grab the reader's attention and convince him or her to go on reading. A good letter might open with a sentence like, "Your innovative designs in office furniture demonstrate that you are concerned with increasing comfort as well as expanding your market," or "Your commitment to quality has inspired me to make the same commitment to myself and to my work."

3. *Give the reader a glimpse of what you can do.* You want to make the reader curious enough to hear more about you. Let the prospective interviewer know what line of work you're in, a general idea of your experience, and how you could apply that experience to the company. You might say, "As a research-and-design expert with eight years of experience in office-furniture design, I am continually increasing my knowledge of ergonomics and improving quality and comfort. I do so in practical, profitable ways."

4. *List two of your accomplishments.* You want to make someone an offer he can't refuse; you want the response to your letter to be, "We could certainly

use someone like that around here!" Look over your Arsenal of Accomplishments and include two that relate to this company's particular interests. Be brief and to the point; you don't want to give everything away in the letter—you can always elaborate in the interview. It's not necessary to include the name of your previous employer(s). Once again, you can elaborate on this at the interview.

5. *State your desire to work for this company, and that you'll call on a specific date to set up an interview.* Write with confidence, as if you're expecting a meeting to take place.

Here is a sample of a successful introductory letter:

April 12, 1993

Ms. Kathryn Miller
Vice-President, Research and Design
Dynamic Office Furniture
23 Sullivan Street
Anytown, USA

Dear Ms. Miller:

Your commitment to quality has inspired me to make the same commitment to myself and to my work. As a research-and-design expert with eight years experience in office furniture design, I am continually increasing my knowledge of ergonomics and improving quality and comfort. I do so in practical, profitable ways:

•In 1991, I increased sales of my company's slowest-moving chair over $500,000 by re-

designing the height adjuster so that it was easier
to reach.

•Last year, I suggested and designed a modular
desk, filing cabinet, and computer cart unit
that gained a 15-percent share of the market in
only nine months.

I can bring the same kind of success to you
and your fine organization. I will call you on
April 21 to set up a meeting.

Yours sincerely,
Michael Sloane

HOW WILL A WELL-WRITTEN LETTER AFFECT MY CHANCES OF GETTING AN INTERVIEW?

If you can write an effective letter, you'll be one of the
few instead of one of the many. Most introductory letters
don't say much more than "I need a job. Please hire me.
I'll wait for your call." So if you send a well-written, carefully researched letter, you'll be well ahead of the game—
and you'll be remembered.

DIALING FOR INTERVIEWS

WHAT'S THE NEXT STEP AFTER I SEND MY LETTER?

Notice that the last line of the letter says "I will call
you." This statement is not to be taken lightly. On very
rare occasions, you may get a call from the person who
received your letter; most of the time, however, the recip-
ient will wait for you to call.

PICTURE THIS:

Kathryn Miller receives the letter from Michael Sloane on April 14. She thinks to herself, "This Michael Sloane sounds pretty interesting. We don't have an opening for him right now, but I'll certainly speak to him when he calls." April 21 comes and goes. No call. The letter gets shuffled around for a week or so. Then Ms. Miller clears it off her desk, thinking, "Too bad I never heard from this guy. He probably got a job somewhere else." She drops the letter into her circular file. Meanwhile, Michael Sloane sits at home, unemployed, waiting for the phone to ring. . . .

If you don't show enough interest to call, the employer will think you don't have enough interest in her. Some people may say no to your request for an interview, but if you never make the call, you'll never find out who might have said yes.

WHAT DO I SAY?

In the next section we'll discuss how you get through to the person to whom you've written. We'll also talk about how to deal with a person who wants to interview you when you call, over the phone. The important thing to remember is that it's your attitude that counts the most. If you sound confident and competent, chances are the potential boss will at least give your request for an interview serious consideration.

THE RÉSUMÉ QUESTION

SHOULD I SEND MY RÉSUMÉ WHEN I SEND THE INTRO-DUCTORY LETTER?

If you're observant, you'll notice that nowhere in this

section have I mentioned a résumé. That's because I don't like them. Résumés tell only the bare-bones facts about a person; they are used most often to screen people out after only a cursory glance or two. The introductory letter is a much better approach because you're making a targeted offer with the benefits to the buyer clearly spelled out. Résumés never have the same impact.

DON'T MOST EMPLOYERS EXPECT TO GET A RÉSUMÉ?

In the real world, however, most people still expect to see résumés. When that happens, my advice is to personalize the résumé as much as possible. Based on your research about the job and the company, try to customize your résumé if you can.

There are many good books on the market that demonstrate how to write an effective résumé. Get one and study it. If you're going to use a résumé, it must be structured so that it shows you off in your best light. Like the introductory letter, the résumé is a tool to get you in the door. Yours should be designed so that it emphasizes your strong points and plays down your weaknesses.

SECRET STRATEGY NUMBER 22:
If you have to send a résumé, present an image
of yourself tailored to the employer's needs
and expectations.

HOW DO I CUSTOMIZE MY RÉSUMÉ?

There are three types of résumés, and you should use

the one that will be most effective for you. They are: the chronological, the functional, and the customized.

WHAT IS A CHRONOLOGICAL RÉSUMÉ?

The chronological résumé is the most traditional type, used about 60 percent of the time. It is just what it sounds like—a chronological job history, starting with your most recent employment and working backward. A chronological résumé is best used to *emphasize job continuity,* either from one company to another, or steady advancement within one organization (i.e., working your way up from the mail room to an account executive within the same company).

WHAT IS A FUNCTIONAL RÉSUMÉ?

A functional résumé highlights your accomplishments and abilities and puts your strongest selling points up front. You should use a functional résumé when you're just entering the job market, when you're reentering the job market after a gap of any length, when you're changing careers, or when you've had a number of unrelated jobs.

WHAT IS A CUSTOMIZED RÉSUMÉ?

The customized résumé is the most job specific, and the one I recommend most. This résumé is personalized for the particular job so that your accomplishments and the requirements of the job match up as closely as possible. This type of résumé always begins with a job objective, written specifically to suit this job. This takes time, because you have to change your résumé for every inter-viewer (or at least for type of job, i.e., if you are pursuing both industrial design and commercial art, you'd change your job objective and highlighted accomplishments for each pursuit), but it makes it easier for a prospective employer to "put you in his picture"—to see how you would fit into this job. This is also the best résumé to use if you don't have much work experience or if you've changed jobs several times.

HOW DO I KNOW WHICH IS THE BEST TYPE OF RÉSUMÉ FOR ME TO USE?

There are no hard-and-fast rules for writing résumés. Some of the most effective are combinations of the three formats listed above. However, as with the introductory letter, your résumé's appearance is almost as important as its content. Sloppy reproduction, typographical errors, and/or dirty, wrinkled paper will most likely mean your résumé will go straight to the rejection pile.

CAN I JUST SEND A RÉSUMÉ WITHOUT AN INTRODUCTORY LETTER?

Never send a résumé by itself. It must always be accompanied by a letter to convince the interviewer to read the résumé more carefully and see how your experi-ence and abilities can benefit him and his company.

Introductory letters, telephone marketing, and an effective résumé are the equipment you need to tap into the vast arena of "hidden" interviews. Telephone marketing is one area that gives many people trouble. Therefore, the next section goes into detail about how to make the telephone one of the most effective tools you need for interview success.

SMART QUESTIONS TO ASK ABOUT CALLING THE INTERVIEWER: MAKING THE MOST OF YOUR TELEPHONE CONNECTIONS

Just as death and taxes are inevitable, so is using the telephone as part of the job-search process. No matter how many letters of introduction or résumés you send out, the number of interviews you'll receive is directly proportional to the number of phone calls you make to follow up.

On the rare occasion that an employer does respond directly to a letter you've sent, he (or his assistant) will give you a call. Perhaps you'll get a call from a headhunter. Whatever the circumstance, you'll be on the phone. And whether you're placing or receiving the call, there are definite techniques you can learn to make the telephone your connection to interview success.

FACING THE FEAR OF PHONES

I DON'T KNOW WHY, BUT I HATE MAKING THOSE FOLLOW-UP CALLS. IS THIS UNUSUAL?

There is a phenomenon called "phone phobia" that attacks many of us just as we are about to pick up the phone to make those important calls. The fear of rejection suddenly hits. What if the person on the other end says no to your request for an interview? It might happen. In fact, it probably will happen. Not everyone you contact is going to be receptive.

In order to get over this fear and obtain the interviews you want, you've got to rely on the law of averages: the more calls you make, the higher your average return. You have to expect that you will get a certain percentage of rejections. But those who say yes will be people who are truly interested in what you have to say.

ARE THERE OTHER CAUSES, BESIDES THE FEAR OF REJECTION, FOR PHONE PHOBIA?

You may be embarrassed to call. You may assume that you're interrupting someone's busy schedule, using up their valuable time. The truth is that your time is valuable as well, and that you are calling with an offer of great value—YOU!

Your skills, talents, and experience might be just what the person on the other end of the phone needs. You must believe this yourself, or the person to whom you're speaking won't believe it either.

If you're still concerned about making that first call, remember that when you do, you have several advantages over the person at the other end:

- You know more about the person you're speaking to than she knows about you. You know there's a strong possibility she'll be interested in speaking with you. You may know some of her problems, and have come up with ways to offer your assistance. She'll probably be impressed with your knowledge and preparation for the call.
- The person to whom you're speaking is not prepared for your call. On the other hand, you have spent a long time preparing for it; therefore, you'll be ready to handle any objection or answer any question she may have.
- You have a strong objective in mind (getting an interview), which gives you the edge in the situation.
- The person on the other end is being asked to make a quick and unexpected decision. The only decision you have to make is what to say next.

WHEN I'M CALLING FROM HOME, IT'S HARD TO FEEL LIKE I'M A PROFESSIONAL. WHAT CAN I DO ABOUT THAT?

First, make sure that you're physically comfortable using the phone. Dress for the part. If you don't want to wear a suit to make the calls, at least wear something other than jeans. And *never* make job-related calls in your pajamas or robe. Try to set a separate work area for yourself so you'll feel more professional. Make sure that your work area is well stocked with pens and paper, as well as an appointment calendar and copies of the letters you sent out.

SECRET STRATEGY NUMBER 23:
When making phone contact with a potential interviewer, you're calling as one professional

to another—let your manner and attitude reflect your professionalism.

I'M PRESENTLY EMPLOYED AND LOOKING FOR A NEW JOB. CAN I MAKE CALLS FROM MY DESK?

Don't make calls from the office during work time. Use coffee breaks and lunch hours, and be sure to bill your calls to your phone credit card. There are cases, if you've been laid off or let go, when the company will allow you (or even encourage you) to make such calls while you're still on the job. Before you do, make sure that this is the case. Whatever the situation, be sure you behave ethically.

GETTING PAST THE GATEKEEPER OR PROTECTIVE SECRETARY

Let's suppose you've done your homework; you've written letters to the appropriate executives at several different companies. You're about to follow up those letters with the objective of obtaining a face-to-face interview. One common problem you may encounter when trying to get an interview is the fact that the person you wish to speak to is probably not the person who answers the phone. You want to speak directly to the person who has the power to hire; more than likely you will first have to get past the protective secretary.

HOW DO I GET PAST THE PROTECTIVE SECRETARY?

Here are some methods you can use to get past the gatekeeper:

METHOD NUMBER 1: *Stay (politely) on course.* When you call and the secretary answers, immediately state to whom you wish to speak: "Ronald Jones, please." Don't ask a question or even have a question in your voice; assume you'll be put right through. A good secretary will be doing her job—and part of that job is screening the boss's calls.

If the secretary asks, "What is this in reference to?" you can reply, "Mr. Jones is expecting my call." This is true, because you wrote in your letter that you would follow up with a phone call. This usually gets you through immediately.

METHOD NUMBER 2: *Candor.* If the secretary is being particularly difficult, the worst thing you can do is argue or become defensive. You may want to try the direct approach and say, "I know that you're doing your job and trying to protect your boss's time. But he is expecting my call, and this will only take a minute or two of his time."

METHOD NUMBER 3: *Develop a relationship.* A secretary can be a great source of information—about the company and about the boss. Try to build a relationship with the secretary so that the next time you call you will be put through quickly. Write down the secretary's name. If you call back again, be sure to use the name in your conversation. Secretaries often have a great deal of influence with their bosses. If you do get through by being rude or devious, the secretary will certainly remember this and can very well keep you from being hired.

METHOD NUMBER 4: *Call early; call late.* If the boss isn't available, ask the secretary for a specific time to call back. Find out if the boss usually comes in early or stays late. It's better to call back again than to leave a message.

Method Number 5: *The technological approach.* Nowadays you may never even reach a secretary; you may simply reach a voice-answering system. You dial the extension of the person to whom you want to speak, and you get a computerized voice saying, "Mr. Jones is not in at the moment. Please leave a message after you hear the beep." Once again, try not to leave a message. Most systems have an escape clause—when you first call, the computer will say, "If you have a rotary phone, or do not know the extension, please hold the line." Then a real human will talk to you, and you may be able to find out information about the boss's schedule.

If you keep calling and can never get through, try rehearsing an attention-getting message to leave the next time you call. Use your introductory letter as the basis for your script. You might say something like, "This is Michael Sloane calling for Ronald Jones. I sent you a letter last week describing my eight years experience in industrial design and the valuable contribution I know I could make to your organization. I'm sorry that I haven't been able to reach you; please call me at 555-1213. If I don't hear from you within a week, I will try you again."

Method Number 6: *Make the telephone operator your personal secretary.* Another way to get through to the decision maker is to use a person-to-person call. Though this can be time-consuming and expensive, it does work. Person-to-person calls don't have to be long-distance; you can use this system to make local calls. Tell the operator you want to make a person-to-person call to Mr. Jones, and you will speak only to Mr. Jones. Instruct the operator that if Mr. Jones is not in, please leave a message that you called person-to-person. After two or three of these calls, Mr. Jones's curiosity will be whetted and he'll probably return your call.

SECRET STRATEGY NUMBER 24:
Every time you make a call, your goal is to
get through to the decision maker.

WHEN IS THE BEST TIME TO MAKE THESE CALLS?

Most executives' schedules change from day to day and unexpected situations always arise. Even if a secretary tells you to call back at 2:30, the boss may not be there. She may have been called to handle an emergency or attend an impromptu meeting. Often the best times to connect with busy people are before work, during lunch, and after work. If the workday starts at nine, call at 8:30 or 8:45. Try at 12:15 and 12:45, then again at 5:15 and 5:30. You might even try on Saturday mornings, when many executives come in to catch up on extra work, and the gatekeeper is not around to take their calls.

THE PREINTERVIEW INTERVIEW

WHAT HAPPENS WHEN I FINALLY DO GET THROUGH TO THE DECISION MAKER? OR WHEN A PROSPECTIVE EMPLOYER CALLS ME IN RESPONSE TO A LETTER I SENT?

It's very rare that anyone will say, "I got your letter; come in for an interview tomorrow." More likely, a preinterview, or screening, will take place over the phone.

HOW DO I HANDLE A SCREENING INTERVIEW?

No one has ever been hired as a result of a screening interview alone, but many people have been rejected because of it. So you must be thoroughly prepared, proceed with confidence, and go directly after your objective—the face-to-face interview.

Always begin by using the employer's name, either by saying, "Is this Kathryn Miller?" or "Is this Ms. Miller?" If she answers her line by saying her name, repeat it anyway, followed immediately by your name and the fact that you sent her a letter. You don't want her to spend time on the phone trying to figure out who you are.

HOW DO I GO ABOUT GETTING AN APPOINTMENT?

Once you've introduced yourself and reminded her of your letter, take a deep breath and go for it. Start right in with a powerful accomplishment, then request an appointment: "Kathryn Miller? This is Michael Sloane. I'm the R&D executive who wrote you a letter last week saying that I designed a new home-office unit that gained a 15-percent share of the market in nine months. I know I could be of similar benefit to your company. I can come in and see you on Wednesday the twenty-eighth at quarter to three or Thursday the twenty-ninth at quarter to ten. Which would be best for you?"

SECRET STRATEGY NUMBER 25:
When calling for an interview appointment,
set up the expectation that there *will be* a meeting.
Give the prospective interviewer a choice between
two times.

WHY DO I NEED TO SUGGEST THE TIME FOR THE MEETING?

There are several reasons for you to suggest the appointment times. First, you set up the expectation that there will be a meeting. You're giving the prospective interviewer two choices, neither of which is *not* to see you.

Second, you don't want to give the impression that your schedule is completely free and that you can meet with her at her beck and call (even if this is true). By giving her exact times, it makes it easy for her to look right at her calendar for an opening, and implies that you have a busy schedule to keep as well.

Third, by saying that you can come at quarter to the hour, you take the pressure off her having to schedule you in for an entire sixty minutes. She may not have an hour to spare. But if you use the quarter hour, the assumption is that the interview will only be fifteen minutes long.

WHAT DO I DO IF SHE SAYS NO?

Unfortunately, the road to getting an interview is hardly ever smooth. You will need to be persistent, and keep your objective in mind as you go. You should be prepared for all kinds of responses. Here are a few of the objections, or stumbling blocks, you may encounter, and suggestions for getting around them. (These are typical objections and suggested responses. Don't try to memorize these answers; they are meant to give you an idea of how to handle such situations.):

> OBJECTION: "I never received your letter."
> REPLY: "I'm sorry you haven't seen it. But I would be happy to tell you more about myself Tuesday morning or Wednesday afternoon. Which would be better for you?"

Objection: "Why don't you just send a résumé?"

Reply: "I'd be glad to, Mr. Jones. Is this the correct address—1633 Broadway? I'll send it out today. But just to be sure I'd be right for your company, what particular skills or qualifications would make someone well suited to be a member of your team?" (That way you agree with the employer's request, then reopen the conversation and give yourself a chance to pursue your objective once more.)

Objection: "Everyone we hire must go through personnel."

Reply: "I understand. Is there a particular person I should speak to there? Is there a specific job or title I should mention?" (Ideally, you want to be able to call personnel and say, "Mr. Jones recommended I call you regarding the assistant manager's position in the research-and-design department." The employer's answer also lets you know whether or not there is an actual position open, or if the employer is simply passing you on.)

Objection: "Before I talk to you, I'd like to know what kind of salary you're looking for."

Reply: If there's any way at all of avoiding this answer, find it. If you ask for too much, you may knock yourself out of the running. If you give a low figure, the employer may assume you don't have enough experience, or don't know the market well enough. Say something like, "The most important thing to me right now is to find the right company and the right person to work for. I know your company's reputation, and I'm sure you would compensate me fairly. I'd be glad to discuss this with you further in person, either Tuesday afternoon or Wednesday morning. Which is better for you?"

HOW SHOULD I END THE CONVERSATION?

You can never know all the factors that go into the employer's decision. So if you do get a no, don't take it personally. Remember to network. Ask if there is anyone else in the company (if it is large enough) or anyone else the employer knows who might benefit from your services.

If you get a yes, good for you! Repeat all the details of the interview setup back to the employer. Make sure you have the correct address, and the right date and time. If you need directions, ask for them (or call back and ask the receptionist or secretary). Then say good-bye and get off the phone. You have nothing to gain by staying on the line after you've accomplished your objective.

You'll have plenty of time to go into greater detail, to answer any further questions, and to ask questions of your own, during the interview.

We will explore some of the questions you should be asking in Section 18. First, however, you need to know what types of questions you will be asked during a typical interview—and how you can use your answers to sell yourself and get the job of your choice.

SMART QUESTIONS TO ASK ABOUT ANSWERING TOUGH QUESTIONS: HOW TO REVEAL THE SKELETONS IN YOUR CLOSET WITHOUT TALKING YOURSELF OUT OF A JOB

Have you ever been fired from a job? Have you ever applied for a position for which you were not qualified (according to the formal job description)? Were you ever told at a job interview that you were overqualified? Did you ever decide *not* to go on a job interview because you were afraid the interviewer would ask you questions you just didn't know how to answer?

If so, you are not alone.

It is very rare that you will apply for a job for which you are *perfectly* suited. And you will be asked tough questions at every interview, there's no doubt about that. However, by studying a few basic principles about how to answer tough questions, and by practicing these techniques beforehand, you can learn how to handle yourself well under the "worst" of circumstances.

233

SELL YOURSELF INTO A JOB

Before you go into any interview, review the principles of selling yourself discussed in Section 4. Remember the reason a person buys any product: there has to be something in it for him. The boss wants to know how hiring you will benefit him. With every tough question you answer, you have another chance to sell yourself, to restate your case, to show the "buyer" the real value he is getting for his money.

WHEN AN INTERVIEWER ASKS ME TOUGH QUESTIONS, I ALWAYS FEEL AS THOUGH HE'S TRYING TO TRICK ME IN SOME WAY. AM I RIGHT ABOUT THAT?

Although it may feel that way from your point of view, an interviewer doesn't ask you so-called tough questions to trick you or trip you up, nor does he enjoy making you feel uncomfortable. He can find out your basic qualifications by reading your résumé, but that doesn't tell him if you're reliable, if you can handle pressure situations, if you can communicate well, or if you'll fit in with the rest of the team. Questions are the only tool he has to find out what kind of person you really are.

SO WHAT IS AN INTERVIEWER REALLY LOOKING FOR WHEN HE'S ASKING QUESTIONS?

Every employer has an ideal candidate in mind. That fictional person has just the right background and experience, will fit in with the team, and can help solve the employer's problems.

When employers ask you tough questions, they're

measuring you against their ideal candidate. They want you to fit as closely as possible; they're really hoping that you'll show them the reasons they should hire you for the job. Suppose a boss says, "We're looking for someone with three to four years of experience in the field. What makes you think you can handle the job?" You might take that as a rejection, and think you have no chance at the job. But what she's really saying is, "I'd like to give you a chance, but you don't match my *ideal* candidate's description. Show me how you can make up for the lack of experience."

HOW DO I KNOW IF I'VE ANSWERED A QUESTION CORRECTLY?

An interview is not a test. There are no right or wrong answers. There are only your answers. And the more questions you are asked, the better off you are. An interviewer doesn't continue to ask you questions unless he is interested in you. If he's not, he'll end the interview early with a variation on "Don't call us, we'll call you."

If he is interested, he'll ask you more questions. And each question you're asked means another chance to get the job.

SECRET STRATEGY NUMBER 26:
Every question you are asked provides you with another opportunity to sell yourself.

HOW DO I TURN A TOUGH QUESTION INTO AN OPPORTUNITY TO SELL MYSELF?

Suppose you were fired from your last job. The

prospective boss asks you, "Why did you leave your previous position?" Although you may think this is a skeleton in your closet you would never want revealed, you can use it to your advantage (besides, you can't lie about being fired; if the prospective boss finds out, you won't get the job anyway).

If you are not prepared for the question, you might blurt out, "My supervisor wouldn't answer any of my questions. Then when my project failed, she blamed me." That may be what happened, but your answer does nothing to further your cause, or answer the employer's hidden question, "Why should I hire you?"

If you're prepared for the question you could answer, "My supervisor and I had some difficulties communicating. Looking back on it now, I see that there are ways I might have handled myself differently. As a matter of fact, the experience taught me a lot, and I now know how to handle myself in a much more professional manner."

This type of answer shows the prospective boss that you are willing (and able) to learn from your mistakes and to accept your share of responsibility for a difficult situation. These are desirable qualities in a job candidate.

HOW DO I KNOW WHAT THE BOSS'S NEEDS AND CONCERNS ARE SO THAT I CAN ADDRESS THOSE CONCERNS IN MY ANSWER?

You do that by asking questions as well as answering them. In the next section, we'll go over the kinds of questions you should be asking.

Another way is to be sure that you answer the question the boss is really asking. Suppose you're asked the question "Can you work under pressure?" This is a definite candidate for a clarifying question. Ask the interviewer to explain what he means by pressure. It may turn out that this is an extremely high-pressure job, involving tight deadlines and lots of overtime. You might decide you don't want such a job. Or, it might turn out that the interviewer's idea of pressure is tame compared with the pressure of your previous job, and you would have no trouble working under these conditions. Remember Secret Strategy Number 12: Never answer an interviewer's question unless you're 100 percent certain you know what it means.

QUESTIONS YOU DON'T HAVE TO ANSWER

DO I HAVE TO ANSWER EVERY QUESTION WHEN IT'S ASKED?

If a question makes you uncomfortable, or if you'd like time to think about your answer, you can always try a diversionary tactic. You can say, "That's a good question, Ms. Taylor, but can I ask you something that just came to mind?"

If you want to answer the question but need time to think, you can say so. "I'd like to think about that question a bit, Ms. Taylor. Can we come back to it later?" Or just take a minute or so to think about it. We tend to think of silence as the enemy and feel a great need to fill up every minute. But if you need time to think, take it and give the best answer you can.

AREN'T THERE SOME TYPES OF QUESTIONS THAT AN EMPLOYER CANNOT LEGALLY ASK?

The Equal Opportunity Commission has strict laws

about questions pertaining to age, criminal record, financial affairs, handicaps, national origin, marital or family status, race or color, religion, or sex.

If you feel that questions being asked in any of these areas are not directly related to job requirements, you can legitimately—but politely—refuse to answer. You might say, "Before I answer that question, can you tell me how it specifically relates to this job?" If you don't get a satisfactory answer, you probably don't want to work for this person anyway.

TOUGH QUESTIONS, SMART ANSWERS

Here are some tough questions you may be asked during any interview. Do not try to memorize any of the answers suggested here. They are provided only to give you an idea of why such a question is being asked, and to give you an example of a sales-oriented answer.

- *Why did you decide to go to the university you attended?* This is a question that is usually asked when you are just out of school, or have little experience working. Most of the time, the interviewer is less concerned with *which* college you attended than with *how* you made the decision to go there. She wants to follow your reasoning process, see how you make evaluations, and find out how you come to difficult decisions.
- *When you were in school, did you participate in school activities? What were they, and why did you choose them?* Once again, it's not what you chose that's important, it's why you chose them. If you were on the bridge team, for instance, let the employer know

what excited you about the game—and how the personal qualities it takes to be a bridge champion
relate to the qualities you need to succeed on the
job.

•*How do you spend your spare time? What are your
hobbies?* This is similar to the question above. The
interviewer isn't trying to pry into your private life;
he wants to find out about the real you. If you say
that you spend all your free time watching old
movies on TV, you may not be showing yourself off
in the best light. It's okay to be a movie buff; just
don't paint a picture of yourself sitting passively
watching films. Talk about your knowledge of films,
your passion and enthusiasm, how you organized a
film society in your community. . . . Again, find ways
of relating what you bring to your hobby to what
you could bring to this job.

•*Why is it that you've been unemployed for over a year
now?* Employers know how bad the situation is, and
how tough it is to get a job today. The interviewer is
probably asking this question to find out how you'll
handle the answer. Whatever you do, don't get
defensive. You might say, "I'm sure you know how
difficult the situation is. There have been some jobs
I wanted that I didn't get. But I am also looking for a
job that I really want, one that I can feel committed
to. I believe I can make the best contribution to a
company by being happy at what I do. I'm not willing
to take just any job and perform poorly in it because
I'm not really suited for it. This seems to be a job for
which I am suited, and I'm prepared to give my best
in both attitude and performance." This answer
shows you to be serious, honorable, and concerned
about doing well for the company.

•*What have you been doing during all this time of*

unemployment? The obvious answer is, "I've been looking for work." But the interviewer knows you can't look for work twenty-four hours a day. She wants to know if you've been sitting around feeling sorry for yourself, or if you've spent the time productively. Talk about any part-time or consulting work you've done. Let her know about your association memberships, and your committee activities, and/or about any volunteer work you've been doing. Perhaps you've been able to go back to school, or to take courses to better yourself. Emphasize the fact that you have been keeping up, or improving, your skills while you've been out of work.

- *What have you learned from some of the previous jobs you've held?* The interviewer is looking for the large picture here. If you can, talk about what you learned about the industry as a whole, or about the specific profession. "I learned that being an accountant means more than crunching numbers. It means paying great attention to detail at the same time you're looking at the overall problem" or "I learned that the bottom line is not an accountant's only concern. I must be able to communicate my findings, and often my processes, to my supervisors and coworkers." Tie your answers into qualities you know the interviewer admires (which you've discovered by asking your own questions).

- *Why do you want to work for our company?* This is a perfect opportunity for you to let the employer know you did your homework. Relate your answer specifically to the company's product or service. "I've used your word-processing software for years, and especially admire the most recent upgrade of that program. I know that with my marketing expertise, and my background in the travel industry, I could expand sales of this system to travel-related companies nationwide."

Tap into the corporate culture, or the shared values of its employees. "I truly admire the way that this company has been in the forefront of environmental awareness. The 'Save the Trees' community project you started inspired many other companies to follow suit. I'm sure I, too, would be inspired to do my best for a company with that philosophy."

- *Tell me about yourself.* This is the classic interview opener. You want to use this opportunity to sell yourself, not to tell your life story. You need more information before you can answer. You can counter this statement with, "There's so much I could tell you, but I want to be sure to focus on what's important to you. What specifically would you like to know?" The more general the question, the more important it is that you ask a clarifying question.

- *Can you tell me about any hardships or unusual difficulties you had to overcome to reach your goals?* The problem itself isn't as important as your specific approach to it. Talk about how you normally go about solving problems, and then give an example. You might say, "The first thing I do when I recognize a problem is write it down. I make a list of all my options in dealing with the problem, and the possible consequences of each option. Then I choose the one that seems most appropriate for the situation. For instance, a few months ago our entire computer system went down in the middle of compiling a new-product presentation. I thought of postponing the meeting, but then decided that we could get the job done by sending it out to free-lancers to complete. The job was done and the meeting went forward as scheduled. We got the account—and $3 million worth of new business."

A word of caution: Never use an example of a problem you had with an individual coworker or supervisor. You don't want to be seen as someone who has difficulty getting along with others.

•*Do you prefer working with others or by yourself?* If you answer this question without knowing anything about the job itself, you're probably in for trouble. (This is true about most of the questions you'll be asked. That's why you need to ask questions of your own.)

This question is usually asked to determine whether or not you are a team player, but it may also be asked to determine whether or not you can work independently. Ask a clarifying question such as, "Does this job require that I work alone?"

Or you might say, "If this job is like most others, there are times when I'll need to work alone and times when I'll need to work with others. I actually enjoy both of those situations." Then you could go on to cite a example of a project you did independently, and one in which you were a member of a team.

•*Do you think you would have problems working for a younger man or woman?* The law says that employers can't discriminate against you because of your age. But sometimes they're concerned about bringing "older" workers into departments headed by younger employees. Of course, you want to answer that this situation is no problem for you. If you can, relate an example of how you coped with this situation in a previous job, or in some other area of your life (such as taking an adult-education course taught by a young instructor).

•*What did you like about your last job? What did you dislike about it?* It would be best not to answer this question until you have sufficient information about the job for which you are applying. If you haven't been given that information, you might try a diversionary tactic: "Before I answer that, I'd like to ask a question that just came to mind."

Once you know what this job entails, you can come back to this question and relate the things you liked about your last job to the requirements and personal characteristics necessary for success on this job.

Once again, don't dwell on the negative. You don't want to sound like there was nothing you disliked about your job (if that was true, you wouldn't be leaving), but talk about the large-picture reasons. "The only thing I didn't like was that I was working for such a small company. There was no room for growth; I'm really looking for the opportunities a larger company can provide."

- *What was the last book you read (or movie you saw)? How did it affect you?* This is another attempt to find out about the "real you." Don't answer with the latest trendsetter or book on business success just because you think that might impress the interviewer. You don't have to answer with the last book you read—choose your favorite book or movie. Try to chose something with a positive message or an uplifting theme.

- *What have you done that shows initiative?* Initiative is an important quality to many employers. They're looking for people who can think for themselves and make decisions when necessary. Go through your Arsenal of Accomplishments and find an example of a time you took the initiative and saved your company money, brought in new business, increased productivity, etc.

- *What would you do if you disagreed with your supervisor?* This kind of question is an attempt to discover how you handle potentially unpleasant situations. You might want to answer something like, "If we were in a conversation or a meeting where the supervisor asked my opinion, I would give it, even if I disagreed. However, if we were in a meeting where my opinion was not asked, I would not give it right then. I would ask to see the supervisor after the meeting or later that day and express my concerns." This shows that you are not afraid to disagree, that you will stand up for what you think, and that you can do so in an appropriate manner.

- *What would you do if you disagreed with a new company policy that had been instated?* The purpose here is the same as for the question above. The employer wants to know if you'll stand up for your beliefs, but he also wants to find out if you're a potential troublemaker. A good answer, especially if you're being considered for a managerial position, might be, "My first reaction would be to support the company, and I would do so in front of my staff. However, I would then question my superiors, find out why the policy is being instated, and voice my objections."

- *Do you see this paper clip on my desk? Can you sell it to me?* This type of question used to be asked only of salespeople and telemarketers. But more and more employers are asking all job candidates to sell them something because it shows how quickly people can think on their feet and how well they can communicate.

  If you find yourself in this situation, remember the concepts of benefit selling. A customer will buy only when you answer the question, "What's in it for me?" Start out by asking a question to determine how paper clips can solve the interviewer's problems. "What is it about having loose papers on your desk that concerns you?" Then answer those concerns, and end with a closing question (one that will help you make the sale): "I can send you a dozen boxes of clips immediately. Which would you prefer, the silver or the assorted colors?"

- *Give an example of leading a team to a specific objective and how you achieved it.* This is obviously designed to see if you have leadership abilities. It's also designed to see if you're a team player. Use an example in which you were a project leader or supervisor, but don't leave out the contributions of the rest of the people involved.

- *If you were a project leader or director, how would you handle disciplinary problems?* This is a question that definitely needs clarification. What does the interviewer mean by "disciplinary problems"? If he's referring to poor performance, you don't want to relate your answer to sexual harassment. The worst thing you can say is that you'd call personnel and let them work it out. The interviewer wants to know that you can handle problems yourself, in a fair and judicious manner.

- *Where might accounting (or advertising or retailing or any industry or job) fail to meet your needs and how would you compensate?* Once again, try to stay away from negatives as much as possible. Let the interviewer know how accounting (or any of the others) *will* meet your needs. Then add, "No one area of my life can cover all my needs. That's why I enjoy playing tennis—so I can fulfill my needs for physical exercise and friendly competition."

- *I'm not sure you have the experience (or training) for this job. Do you think you can handle it?* The employer is giving you a perfect opportunity to sell yourself with this question. He's asking you to help him find a solution to the problem that you don't have enough experience. Look for benefits you have that others (even those with more experience) may not possess.

- *Where do you see yourself five years from now?* What this question really means is, "Are you going to be around for the long haul? Or do you see this job as a stepping-stone for your next career move?" Let the employer know that you anticipate being very happy in this job. Sell your sense of commitment and find examples of your record of loyalty and reliability. There's no need to pretend that you're not interested in promotion, however. Some positions are logical foundations for career growth. If this is a position from which previous employees have been promoted, you will probably do the same.
- *What sort of money are you looking for?*

SECRET STRATEGY NUMBER 27:
Never talk money until you know there is a job offer.

If you're asked this question early on in the interview, you might say, "I prefer not to discuss money until I know more about the job, and you know whether or not I'm right for it." Or, you can say, "I'm more concerned about finding the right job and the right employer. What is the salary range for this position?" (If at all possible, you want to get the employer to mention a dollar figure first.)

- *How much money were you making on your previous job?* This is a tougher question to evade. If you can't get out of answering, don't lie. The employer may ask you for verification, such as a pay stub or tax return. You can always say that you prefer not to supply such personal information. However, as in the question above, try to turn the tables and ask what the job pays before you answer any such question.

You might avoid answering this question by saying something like, "What is important here is not what I earned in the past, but whether or not I can help you now and in the future. I'm sure that this company wants to compensate people fairly."

If you want to sell yourself effectively into a job, you need to do more than answer questions asked of you. The questions you ask the employer are also selling tools. You can't make a sale without asking questions. You want to ask questions to uncover the employer's needs and wants; you want to ask questions to find the emotional reasons the prospective boss might have for hiring you. The next section explores the kinds of questions you might want to ask, and what you hope to discover by asking them.

SECTION 18

SMART QUESTIONS TO ASK ABOUT GETTING THE INFORMATION YOU NEED: QUESTIONS YOU SHOULD BE ASKING AT EVERY INTERVIEW

Who has more power in an interview situation: the prospective employer or the job applicant?

This is a trick question.

The answer is that neither party has more power. What's involved here is a meeting between two professionals, one with a service to offer and one with a problem to solve. It's important to keep this equality factor in mind. It can make all the difference in whether or not you are offered a job.

You will find that your nervousness about interviews decreases in direct proportion to the amount of preparation and practice you put into interviewing skills. Before every interview, reread your notes concerning the job, the company, and the employer. Go over your Arsenal of

Accomplishments and pick out achievements of particular relevance to this position.

Most of your interview time should be spent asking questions and listening to the answers. You don't want to be speaking endlessly about yourself without having any idea of what the other person wants to hear. Your questions also give the employer clues about your interest level and preparation. You will be judged not only by the answers you give to an interviewer's question, but by the quality of your questions as well.

THE TWO-OBJECTIVE INTERVIEW

Most people think there's only one objective to an interview—and that is to get a job offer. They're wrong. There is a second, equally important objective, and that is to get information about the job and the company.

SECRET STRATEGY NUMBER 28:
There are two objectives to every interview:
1. Get a job offer.
2. Get as much information as possible
about the job, the boss, and the company.

DO I ALWAYS WANT TO GET A JOB OFFER, EVEN IF I'M NOT IMMEDIATELY SURE I WANT THE JOB?

You can always say no to a job offer; it's your decision. But without a lot of information from your prospective boss, how will you know whether or not this is a job you want to take? That's why you must remember that you're not only going to be interviewed, you are also going to interview the boss.

WHO ASKS MORE QUESTIONS, ME OR THE PROSPECTIVE BOSS?

No one is keeping track of how many questions either of you is asking. However, you do want to be sure that you're not the only one who is talking. In *Your Hidden Assets: The Key to Getting Executive Jobs,* Orrin G. Wood, Jr., says, "Your strategy is to get the interviewer to do most (perhaps two-thirds) of the talking. . . . One of your more effective tools is asking intelligent questions. Not only can it prompt the interviewer to give you direction as to what he or she is interested in, it can also relieve tension if the interviewer is probing a sensitive area or an area you would rather defer until later."

Every interview is a question-and-answer session, with both sides trying to get the information they need within a limited time frame. An ideal interview should be give and take, with each person asking and answering questions.

HOW DO I GET THE INFORMATION I NEED?

If you want to get information from your interviewer, you're going to have to ask questions. There's no need to be obnoxious, pushy, or overbearing during this process. What you want to do is take an active role in the interviewing process.

Employers want to see your energy, to know that you are willing and able to express your own ideas and show some initiative. An interview is really a sales process—

you're selling yourself, your skills, and your ability to do the job—and you want to make the sale. In order to do that, you've got to take control. To take control, you've got to ask questions.

HOW DOES ASKING A QUESTION PUT ME IN CONTROL?

When you ask a question, you steer the conversation in the direction you want it to go. The more questions you ask, the more control you have.

SECRET STRATEGY NUMBER 29:
Each time you answer an employer's question,
regain control by asking another question.

For instance, if any employer asks you, "Why do you think you're qualified for this job?" follow your answer with, "What would you most like for a new employee to bring to this position?"

Before the interview, make a list of questions you would like to have answered. Always use open-ended questions that require more than a yes-or-no answer. For instance, don't ask, "Did the person who previously held this job quit?" Instead, ask, "Why is this position open?"

IN THE LAST SECTION, THE EMPHASIS WAS ON SELLING MYSELF THROUGH ANSWERS TO THE BOSS'S QUESTIONS. HOW CAN I SELL MYSELF BY ASKING QUESTIONS?

Each time you ask a question, you get more insight into how the interviewer thinks and what is important to her. Suppose you ask, "What would you most like for a new employee to bring to this job?" and the boss answers, "I need someone who can handle high-pressure situations. We're often up against tight deadlines, and I need someone who is levelheaded and organized."

Your next step is to sell yourself as someone who can fill those needs and relieve the boss of her worries. Think about your accomplishments; find one that is appropriate and relate it to the interviewer. You might say something like, "That's great, because I know how to work under those conditions. At my last job, I supervised three simultaneous projects by hanging a large calendar in my office with each step and its due date marked off. My system increased production by 30 percent, and I was able to get all three projects done early."

QUESTIONS YOU MAY WANT TO ASK

Here are some questions you may want to ask prospective employers, and the reasons for asking them:

• *What are the key responsibilities of this job?* This question should provide you with two areas of information. First, you can find out exactly what the job entails. From that information, you can decide whether or not you have the appropriate skills for this job (or feel you can learn them), and if it is the kind of job you would like. Next, by listening carefully to the interviewer, you can glean what is important to him. Suppose he answers, "The key responsibilities of this job are supervising two part-time telemarketers, generating sales leads, and creating and distributing monthly sales reports."

People tend to list the responsibilities in order of their importance; in this case you might want to follow up his answer with an accomplishment involving supervising and managing skills. If you're stronger in one of the others areas mentioned, you could highlight your ability to generate leads or to create reports.

- *What changes or improvements would you like to see in this job?* This is a good opportunity to hone in on an employer's "wish list." Oftentimes, when you ask about the key responsibilities of the job, the boss will tell you what the previous employee did. By asking this follow-up question, you may get him to reveal what the responsibilities of this job should be, not what they've been in the past.

- *What do you foresee as possible obstacles or problems I might have?* The answer to this question can be very revealing. It's perfect for generating an opportunity to sell yourself—let the boss know you have the skills and the experience to turn those problems around and create solutions. On the other hand, this question might give you valuable insight about the inner workings of the company. If the boss answers, "Well, you may have problems with the head of Accounting; he and I don't always see eye to eye when it comes to project development," this could be a warning that the glowing picture of innovative thinking and unlimited project resources the boss has been painting is not quite the company's reality.

- *Of the people who have had this job before, what were the characteristics of those who performed well? Of those who didn't?* You want to find out if you have the qualifications for success in this particular job and company. If one of those characteristics is great attention to detail—and that's definitely not your strong point—you may not want to accept this position. Think like the boss. Let him know in what ways you resemble the successful employees, and in what ways you differ from the unsuccessful job holders.

• *If you hire me, what would your specific expectations be?* Believe it or not, many employers are unclear about exactly what it is they're looking for. They have a general idea of what the job is and the kind of person they might need to fill it, but they're short on specifics. This question may help them to clarify their own thoughts. It will also give you a better picture of how the job will be structured and whether or not it will meet your needs.

One more note—a question such as this one "forces" the employer to imagine you in the job. Anytime you can paint a picture (or help the boss paint one) of yourself as a member of the team, go for it.

• *What would you most like for a new employee to bring to this job?* There is a big difference between a boss who answers, "I want an employee to bring in lots of sales leads," and one who says, "A new employee should bring in energy and enthusiasm." The first boss has a more bottom-line, business-oriented approach. The second is more interested in personality and attitude. Both answers give you clues about the boss's own style and personality.

• *Why is the position open?* Was the last person fired? Did he quit for personal reasons? Was he promoted? Did he resign due to personality conflicts? If you can find out the real reason (you may not get the whole story, but you can ask), you can catch a glimpse of the inner workings of the company. If there were personality conflicts, it may be an indication of a difficult supervisor or a rigid corporate style. If, however, the person was promoted from that position, there's a possibility you will be, too.

• *How long has the position been open?* When buying a

house, it's often a good idea to ask how long it's been on the market. If it's been on the market for an unusually long time (taking the economy into account), there's probably something wrong with it. The same principle applies to jobs. If the position has been open for several months, ask yourself (and the boss) why.

Another factor to consider—if the position has been open for several months, the interviewer may be under pressure to fill it. If you're available to start immediately, it could be a good selling point.

- *How many people have held this job in the last five years?* If there has been a large turnover, there must be a reason for it. Are the boss's expectations too high? Is he too difficult to work with? Or is this a job that is a stepping-stone to higher opportunities within the organization? If the number of employees in that position seems excessively high, ask the boss why there has been so much turnover.

- *With whom would I be working on this job? Is it possible for me to meet them?* My neighbor, an advertising copywriter, once came to me in utter frustration. After only one and a half months on her new job, she was ready to quit. When I asked her why, she said, "I was interviewed for this job by Ms. Cole. We got along extremely well; I really enjoyed the interview. As it turns out, she's the head of the department—and not one of the people I work with on a daily basis. I don't like my team at all!"

Never take a job simply because you like the interviewer; you may never see her again. Try to find out who you would be working with day to day, and meet them if possible. Also, this is another opportunity for the boss to picture you side by side physically and mentally with rest of the staff.

- *How is job performance evaluated here? How regularly is performance evaluated?* Answers to questions like these can tell you a lot about the corporate culture. In a more formal setting, performance evaluation may be standardized, with quarterly or semiannual reviews and written reports. Smaller companies may have no written standards; they may rely on an individual boss's personal recommendations and timetable for adding responsibilities, increasing wages, and bestowing new titles. If you prefer one system over the other, the answer to this question can influence your decision about whether or not to accept a job if it's offered.

- *How is performance rewarded?* Are there performance-linked bonuses? Are raises given according to merit, or according to length of time at the job? What are the criteria for promotions?

   Do the answers to these questions seem fair and logical to you? Would they give you incentive to work hard and challenge yourself? Companies usually reap the type of performance they reward, so their reward systems can be good indicators of the quality of work they generate.

- *What behaviors are rewarded here?* Is staying late and working overtime rewarded? Does the company like its employees to be visible to the industry and/or the community? Are employees expected to entertain clients? These are just a few of the behaviors that might be rewarded by a favorable performance review.

   You also want to know what is frowned upon in the company: Does a messy desk count against you? Failure to join the company softball team or attend company functions? These are the types of things that, although seemingly trivial, may mean the difference between success and failure on the job.

- *How many women and minorities are in middle-to-upper management?* Is this company *really* an equal opportunity employer? This issue should be important to you whether or not you fit into either of those categories. If there are no women and minorities in high-level positions, this company is wasting its most precious resource—its people.

- *Have you had any major layoffs or cutbacks in the past few years? Do you anticipate any in the near future? If so, how would my job and/or department be affected?* The recession has forced many companies—in fact, entire industries—to lay off thousands of people. Obviously, this company needs someone to fill this position now or they wouldn't be interviewing. However, some stricken industries are seasonal, and hiring spurts are followed by firing spurts. No one can foresee the future, but a history of cutbacks can give you some idea of the stability of the company and/or the industry.

- *Does the company have plans for expansion in the near future?* A company that is expanding may be weathering the recession, if not flourishing in it. It also may be moving entire departments and/or individual employees to new locations. If remaining in your immediate location is an important consideration, you might want to find out the details of the company's plans before you accept a job.

- *What type of training is available for this job?* You can get a good idea of a boss's management style by the type of training she makes available for her people. Some have a "sink or swim" attitude: they throw you right into your responsibilities and expect you to make a go of it however you can (it's never as cut-and-dried as that—managers, or others in the department—are usually available for occasional assistance). Some provide formal training programs, where you go to "school" for several weeks before you actually start work.

Most bosses are somewhere in between. They may give you some formal training, and expect you to pick up the rest along the way. The answer to this question should give you an idea of how accessible this boss will be; whether she has an open-door policy for questions or problems, or whether you will need to look elsewhere for help.

• *How often would I meet with you?* This is another question to determine the boss's accessibility. Some bosses may have a structured policy of having staff meetings once a week or once a month. Some may say, "You can meet with me whenever you feel it's necessary." One style is not necessarily better than the other, but one may appeal to you more.

• *What is the corporate culture here? Can you describe the general atmosphere?* With this question you can learn about the company and the interviewer as well. An interviewer might say, "We're a fairly conservative group, and we work very hard." Another might add, "But I like to make sure that we're not all work and no play, so I organize company sports teams and interdepartment games." If you interviewed with both these people, you will have learned a lot about both the company and the potential employer as well.

• *Why did you join this company?* People usually enjoy talking about themselves. Since you may be working closely with this individual, you want to find out a bit more about what he's really like. You don't want to ask about his personal life, but asking about his professional goals can be quite revealing. If you can find out what turns this person on, what excites him, what he is looking for in his professional life, you can then point out your similarities in goals and passions. Bosses often hire people who are similar to themselves.

• *What is it about this company that keeps you here?* It's one thing to be excited about a job when you first get it; it's another to remain in a job for any length of time. You want to find out if the company is a place that keeps its employees stimulated and challenged, if it offers growth potential, and if employees are satisfied enough to stay on.

Make a list of at least ten questions you would like to ask at your next interview:

1._____
_____
2._____
_____
3._____
_____
4._____
_____
5._____
_____
6._____
_____
7._____
_____
8._____
_____
9._____
_____
10._____
_____

CLOSING THE CASE: ASKING FOR THE JOB

When an interview is coming to an end, and you are sincerely interested in the job, don't just say good-bye and walk out the door. Don't be afraid to ask for the job.

I DON'T WANT TO BE TOO OBVIOUS ABOUT ASKING FOR THE JOB. HOW CAN I BE SUBTLE WHEN ASKING CLOSING QUESTIONS?

You can start by using what is known in sales trade as "trial closes." A trial close is a question that is asked early on in the sales process which will give you an indication of whether or not the customer might buy.

For instance, a computer salesperson might ask a series of questions to determine what kinds of problems the customer expects a new computer to solve. Once he has that information, the salesperson might say, "Our model 500 can solve all of the problems we've discussed, and at a greater speed than any of the others at this price. Is that something that would interest you in a computer?"

Suppose an interviewer asked you, "Can you give me an example of a problem you solved on your last job?" You would answer the question as we discussed in the last section. You would then follow your answer with a question like, "Is that the way you would like to see problems solved on this job?"

IS IT EVER APPROPRIATE TO COME RIGHT OUT AND ASK FOR THE JOB?

You should always ask for the job—the difference is in how you ask the question. Fist, take a clue from your interviewer. If she is a secure, confident person, you can be more blatant. If she is nervous and insecure, you should not come on as strong.

If you are being considered for a sales position, use your sales techniques to ask closing questions. In this case, you're selling your ability to make a sale, and this is a perfect opportunity to show what you can do. You might end your interview by asking, "Is there anything we've discussed today that will keep you from making me an offer?"

WHAT IF THE POSITION I'M INTERVIEWING FOR IS NOT SALES-RELATED?

You always want to leave on a positive note and ask a closing question. Often, an interview ends with the prospective employer saying, "Do you have any other questions?" You can answer that by saying, "We've had an interesting discussion and I know I could make a valuable contribution to your company. Is there anything else I can tell you that would help you make a decision in my favor?"

That question may get the interviewer to tell you her concerns about you. Then you'll know what her objections are and how to deal with them.

Once you've answered any lingering objections, you can ask a closing question such as, "Based on this interview, would you consider me a strong candidate for this job?"

IS THAT MY FINAL QUESTION?

No it isn't. When the interview is finally over, the interviewer may say, "Thanks, we'll let you know." Don't just let it go at that. Repeat your enthusiasm for the job and the company. "I would very much like to be a part of your team. May I call you on Friday for your decision?" You always want to take an active role. You don't want to be sitting by the phone waiting for it to ring. You may not be able to control the decision, but you can often control when and how you get the answer. You also want to let the employer know you are someone who makes a commitment and follows up. Then be sure and call when you say you will.

ONCE AGAIN, THE FOLLOW-UP

HOW DO I KEEP TRACK OF WHAT HAPPENS IN EACH INTERVIEW I GO ON?

Make out a sheet similar to the one below for every interview you get. Fill it out as soon as you get home so that you remember all the details.

INTERVIEW FOLLOW-UP WORKSHEET

Name of interviewer:_____
Title:_____
Address:_____
Phone Number:_____
Date & Time of interview:_____
What I wore:_____
Basic responsibilities of job:_____
_____
Reasons I am well suited for position:_____
_____

Reasons job appealed to me:_____

Reasons job did not appeal to me:_____

Any other important information:_____

What is agreed-upon next step:_____

Follow-up letter sent:_____

WHAT SHOULD I INCLUDE IN THE FOLLOW-UP LETTER TO THE EMPLOYER?

Recap the important points both you and the interviewer mentioned during your meeting. If you met other people during the interview, mention them as well. Let the interviewer know you will call within five days (name the specific date) to get his or her feedback.

WHAT SHOULD I DO IF I CALL BACK AND FIND OUT I DIDN'T GET THE JOB?

When you call back, you may be told that you are not being hired, but that you came in second, or that your résumé is being kept on file for future consideration. If that happens, keep in contact with this employer. If you find newspaper or magazine articles you think would be of interest, send them to her. You never know when another position may open up, and you want to be remembered.

*   *   *,

You may be told that the employer would like you to come back for a second round of interviews, either with her or with other people in the company. Section 19 will give you the tools and techniques you need when you get a second chance.

SMART QUESTIONS TO ASK ABOUT "CALLBACK" INTERVIEWS

Congratulations! You've gone through your first interview, and you're being considered for the job. That may lead to a number of possibilities.

- You may be offered the job.
- You may be asked to come back for a second interview with the same interviewer.
- You may be asked to meet for a second interview outside the office, usually in a restaurant or a bar.
- You may be asked to come back for an interview with someone else in the company.
- You may be asked to come back for a panel-style interview, where several people will see you at once.

If you're invited to participate in any of these options, you are being seriously considered for the job, and you should prepare just as thoroughly as you did for the first interview. Let's take a look at each of these options.

WHEN YOU'RE OFFERED THE JOB

WHAT SHOULD I DO IF I'M OFFERED THE JOB?

Although there may be a great temptation to respond to a job offer by jumping up and down and shouting "Hooray!" it would be best to resist the urge. Instead, express your enthusiasm, but ask for time to think it over. You might say, "Thank you so much for offering me this opportunity. I'm very pleased to have the offer, and would like to get back to you tomorrow [or early next week] with my decision. Shall I call you in the morning or the afternoon?"

I'VE DECIDED NOT TO ACCEPT THE JOB. WHAT DO I SAY?

When you call back, tell the employer that although you appreciate the offer very much, you can't accept because . . . Then give your reason. There may be room for negotiation. For example, suppose you decided to turn down the job because the hours are eight to four, and you have to get your kids to school at 8:30. If you tell the boss that's why you can't accept the job, she may just say, "Oh, that's too bad." On the other hand, she may say, "I think we could work out a flexible schedule so that you could work nine to five. Is that acceptable?" Now it's your decision again as to whether or not you'll accept the job.

I'VE DECIDED TO ACCEPT THE JOB. DO I JUST SAY YES OVER THE PHONE AND LEAVE IT AT THAT?

If you're leaning toward accepting the offer, you want to meet again in person to finalize negotiations for salary and benefits (as opposed to discussing this over the phone). When you call back to accept the position, you can say, "I would be very pleased to work with you and your organization. Would it be possible for me to come in and see you again sometime this week to talk over the details?" We will discuss negotiating tactics in the next chapter.

A SECOND INTERVIEW WITH THE SAME INTERVIEWER

I'VE MADE IT THROUGH THE FIRST CUT. I'M BEING STRONGLY CONSIDERED FOR THE JOB, AND I'VE BEEN ASKED TO COME BACK A SECOND TIME. WHAT DO I DO NOW?

Review your follow-up worksheet from the previous interview. What were the prospective employer's major concerns during the interview? You must have answered them satisfactorily, or you wouldn't have been asked back. However, there may have been other candidates who also fit the bill. At this point, you have made the "semifinals," and the interviewer is probably choosing among two or three candidates.

I KNOW THAT THERE ARE TWO OR THREE OTHER PEOPLE WHO HAVE ALSO BEEN CALLED FOR A SECOND INTERVIEW. WHAT CAN I DO TO STAND OUT FROM THE GROUP?

In all likelihood, all of the semifinalists are equal in terms of ability to meet the employer's needs. What can you do to shine a second time? Be even better prepared than you were the first time. Go back to your Arsenal of Accomplishments and find one or two relevant achievements that you hadn't mentioned at your first interview. Ask more probing and clarifying questions. You've made a good first impression; you don't want to do yourself any damage by telling more than is necessary or answering a question that wasn't even being asked.

SHOULD I REFER BACK TO THE EARLIER INTERVIEW?

Let the interviewer know you've been thinking about what was discussed at your first meeting. For instance, you might say, "When we met last week, you mentioned that you're considering expanding into new territories. I've been doing some research, and found that there are no discount-jewelry outlets in any of the malls south of the city. Since I'm very familiar with that area, I feel I could be instrumental in bringing in new markets."

Use this opportunity to ask any questions you forgot, or didn't get a chance to ask at the first interview. There may be some areas of the job, or the company, you want to find out more about before accepting a job offer.

SECRET STRATEGY NUMBER 30:
Use your "callback" interview to reemphasize
your strong points, and to get in-depth information
about the job, the employer, and the company.

WHEN YOU'RE ASKED TO MEET OUTSIDE THE OFFICE

DO INTERVIEWS ALWAYS TAKE PLACE IN THE OFFICE?

There are occasions when you will be asked to return for a second interview—only this time, you'll be meeting outside the office. It could be that the interviewer is on his way out of town, and may ask you to meet him at the airport departure lounge. On rare occasions, you may be asked to the potential boss's home for dinner. Usually, however, you will find yourself invited for an interview over breakfast, lunch, or dinner.

Robin, a young woman I know, was recently asked to meet her potential employer at 5:30 P.M. at a midtown restaurant. She found out later that the boss liked her very much during the first interview, but felt that she was nervous and stiff. The boss thought that a less formal setting might be better for getting to know each other. After a half hour of talking over dinner, Robin was offered the job.

You can get clues as to what the boss is looking for by noticing the atmosphere of the meeting place. An interview at a four-star restaurant will have a different tone than one at a neighborhood pub.

What are the "rules" for meeting outside the office? There are some simple rules to follow in "meal meeting" situations:

- •Prepare exactly as you would for a meeting in the office, and keep your professionalism intact, whatever the setting.
- •No matter how informal the atmosphere, remember

that you are being judged here—your general demeanor and manners say a lot about you.

- Avoid alcohol as a rule. Studies have shown that stress increases the intoxicating effects of alcohol, and you certainly want to keep your mind clear at all times. If you feel pressured to order a drink, make it a wine spritzer or light beer—and then sip it slowly throughout the meal. Never have more than one drink, even if the interviewer does.
- Avoid smoking. If the interviewer smokes first, you may smoke as well, but don't be the first to light up.
- Order foods that you know and like. Don't use this opportunity to order expensive or exotic items on the menu. Stay away from messy foods with drippy sauces.
- Even if the food is not to your liking, don't send it back or make a fuss. You don't want to imply in any way that you're questioning the interviewer's choice of restaurant.
- Be polite to the waitpersons (as you normally are, of course), even if they are clumsy or the service is terrible.
- Don't offer to pick up the check, or to pay your share. This is a business expense for the interviewer. Even if the check is placed in front of you, ignore it. Eventually the interviewer will take care of it.
- Use this opportunity to observe your prospective employer. Just as she is watching your demeanor and manners, you can watch hers.

WHEN YOU'RE ASKED TO INTERVIEW WITH SOMEONE ELSE IN THE COMPANY

IF I'VE ALREADY HAD AN INTERVIEW WITH ONE PERSON IN THE COMPANY, WHY WOULD I BE ASKED TO MEET WITH SOMEONE ELSE?

It could be company policy. It could mean that the interviewer has two or three "good" candidates, can't make up his mind, and wants another opinion. Or it could mean that the first interviewer liked you very much, but doesn't have final authority to hire you for the job. You are probably being called in the second time to meet the interviewer's supervisor, partner, or associate.

HOW DO I PREPARE FOR THE SECOND INTERVIEW?

Although the first interviewer has probably gone over the important details of your initial meeting, you should prepare as if the second interviewer knows nothing at all about you. In fact, you may be asked some of the same questions you were asked the first time. Don't simply repeat your answers from last time, however. This interviewer may have slightly different needs and concerns, and you want to relate your answers to him if you can.

That doesn't mean you have to be everything to everybody. It means that you need to listen carefully to this interviewer's questions, be sure you use your answers to sell yourself (which means showing how you can meet the "customer's" concerns), and be sure you ask questions of your own. Once again, go over your interview follow-up sheet and use this opportunity to get additional information (or information from another viewpoint).

WHEN YOU'RE ASKED TO COME BACK FOR A PANEL-STYLE INTERVIEW

I'VE BEEN ASKED TO COME BACK FOR A SECOND INTERVIEW IN FRONT OF A SELECTION COMMITTEE. WHAT DOES THIS MEAN?

This means that you will be interviewed by a panel of two or more people at the same time. It's difficult enough to walk into a room and face a total stranger for a job interview. What happens when you walk in and there are three, four, five, or ten strangers facing you all in a row? This situation can be pretty intimidating—unless you're prepared in advance.

That's why it's important to ask, when the interview is being scheduled, "With whom will I be meeting?" If you are told you will be interviewed by a panel, ask to have their names and titles.

SHOULD I FOCUS MY ATTENTION EQUALLY ON ALL THE PANELISTS, OR DIRECT MY ANSWERS TO ONE SPECIFIC PERSON?

If you can, find out who has the actual hiring authority. That way you can focus your attention on the most important person there. However, you don't want to blatantly ignore everyone else there. Make eye contact with everyone in the room. After every answer you give, however, be sure to regain contact with the decision maker.

WHAT HAPPENS IF I CAN'T GET THIS INFORMATION?

Don't be upset. You may just be told, "The panel will consist of three senior supervisors," or "There will be seven members of the faculty present, but I don't know at this time exactly who will be there." Simply treat everyone in the room as if he or she were the decision maker.

WITH SO MANY PEOPLE ASKING ME QUESTIONS, WILL I GET A CHANCE TO ASK QUESTIONS OF MY OWN?

If you are not advised by the panel that you may ask questions, you must take it upon yourself to do so. Like any other interview situation, you must be confident and in control. Use clarifying questions to be sure you understand what is being asked. And don't be afraid to ask questions of your own. You can address them to the group as a whole, or to a specific panel member.

WHAT'S THE BEST WAY TO PREPARE FOR A PANEL INTERVIEW?

Think of it as if it were a presentation or a press conference. Be prepared for a barrage of questions from a variety of sources. What are the main points you want to get across? Study your Arsenal of Accomplishments so that you have examples of past behaviors you can use to demonstrate how you will perform as part of their group.

THIS SEEMS LIKE SUCH AN INTIMIDATING SITUATION. WHAT'S THE BEST WAY TO HANDLE IT?

One of the main purposes of any interview is to establish rapport. This might seem an impossible task in a panel set-up. However, it is not as difficult as it seems. When someone asks you a question, direct your answer toward the asker.

The panelists know that this is a stressful situation. They expect that you will be nervous. But if you are prepared, this situation is easy to handle. Answer the questions honestly and with confidence. Use your sense of humor to break the tension. Keep in mind that you have something very valuable to offer this group, and let them know how confident you are in your ability to contribute to the team.

INTERVIEWING FOR A NEW POSITION WITHIN THE SAME COMPANY

I JUST FOUND OUT THAT MY BOSS IS LEAVING AND THE COMPANY IS HIRING A NEW MANAGER. HOW DO I GO ABOUT APPLYING FOR THE JOB?

Talk to your boss first. Let her know that you're interested in the position, and ask her about the procedure. You might also want to ask such questions as:

- Do you know if I am being considered for the job?
- If not, why not?
- If I'm not being considered for the promotion, is my job secure as it is?
- Who is actually going to hire your replacement? Can you put in a good word for me?

WHAT ARE THE ADVANTAGES AND DISADVANTAGES OF BEING A "KNOWN" QUANTITY?

If, for whatever reasons, you have not been performing up to par lately, this fact will be well known before you ever get to an interview. On the other hand, if you've been doing well, this fact will also be known. You have to take an honest, objective look at yourself when applying for a new job within your present organization. You do have the advantage of knowing more about the job and the company than an outsider does. Use this knowledge as a selling point.

I ENJOY WORKING FOR THIS COMPANY, BUT I'M NOT THRILLED WITH THE JOB I HAVE. HOW DO I GO ABOUT FINDING OUT WHAT'S AVAILABLE HERE?

Use your networking skills. Don't wait for positions to be posted on the bulletin board (but read it anyway, just in case). Talk to secretaries and assistants, as well as department heads, and let them know that you're interested in moving somewhere else.

Suppose you're working in the computer department, but you're really interested in training. Talk to the training department. Show an interest in what they do, and keep your connections going even when there is no job opening. Ask them to keep you in mind the next time there's an opening.

Now that the interview process is almost at an end, there is one more detail to include: what to do when you get the job! You have established yourself as a valuable commodity, and the employer wants you—now is the time to take advantage of your bargaining power. You don't just want to take any job; you want to ensure a fulfilling, financially rewarding future. The next chapter will show you how.

SMART QUESTIONS TO ASK ABOUT NEGOTIATIONS: WHAT TO DO WHEN YOU GET THE JOB OFFER

What's Wrong with This Picture?

You've completed a preliminary and a callback interview for your "dream" job. You established good rapport with both people who interviewed you. The job seems well within your capabilities, yet is challenging enough to make it an exciting prospect. At the end of the second go-round (during which the interviewer told you the salary range for this job was $30,000 to $35,000) the interviewer tells you a decision will be reached within three days.

Two days later, you get a phone call. The interviewer says, "We're happy to inform you that we've made a decision and we're offering you the job. Starting salary is $32,000. Can you begin work next Monday?"

You are thrilled. You practically shout into the phone,

"That's great! That's terrific! I'll be there on Monday!"

Thirty-two thousand was not quite as much as you wanted, but you're so happy to get the job, you figure you'd better take what you can get. Right?

Wrong.

CASH IN YOUR BARGAINING CHIP

It took you a lot of time and effort to get to this point. You've just successfully convinced the interviewer of the valuable contribution you can make to his organization. Don't undermine that effort by selling yourself short.

SECRET STRATEGY NUMBER 31:
When you're offered a job, your bargaining
power is greater than it will ever be.
Use it well and wisely!

WHY IS THIS THE BEST TIME TO NEGOTIATE?

The interviewer has also spent a great deal of time and effort in choosing you as the best candidate. He's already made an investment in you, and he doesn't want to have to begin the job-search process all over again. Therefore, now is the time he's most likely to be willing to negotiate.

WHAT EXACTLY IS NEGOTIATION?

According to Webster's Dictionary, to negotiate is "to bring about through conference, discussion, and compromise; to bring about by mutual agreement." The operative words here are "compromise" and "mutual agreement."

Negotiation is not about winning or losing. It's not a form of intimidation or a game of who's got the power. It is an exercise in logic and a form of problem solving.

I'M NOT A PROFESSIONAL NEGOTIATOR. HOW DO I KNOW I'LL BE ANY GOOD AT IT?

Negotiation is much simpler than most people think it is. We negotiate every day. When two (or more) people decide which restaurant to go to, which movie to see, or who gets to take out the garbage, that's negotiation. Negotiation is about giving yourself (and the other people involved) options. Sometimes you give a little more, sometimes you get a little more.

The same principles apply to job-offer negotiations. A successful negotiation doesn't necessarily mean you get everything you ask for. It means you get those things that are most important to you, and you compromise in areas of lesser significance.

KEEPING YOUR GOALS IN SIGHT

HOW DO I KNOW WHAT TO NEGOTIATE FOR?

Before you begin any negotiation process, you must know what is most important to you. Money isn't everything; we all know this. But because money is so important, we often become blinded by dollar figures—whether they're higher or lower than we had expected—and forget about the many other aspects of job-offer negotiations.

My neighbor's son, Steven, had been looking for work as a marketing director for several months. Then, within one week, he received two job offers from two different companies. Company A was a large established firm with a formal atmosphere and a "traditional" approach to marketing, and they were offering Steven a high-end salary. Company B was a newer, up-and-coming firm. They took a more aggressive approach to marketing, and offered Steven more freedom and autonomy on the job. But they couldn't match the salary of the first company.

Steven came to me for advice. We sat down and went over his goals. It turned out that making a lot of money was not as important to Steven as working in a challenging, creative atmosphere, and a chance to advance his career.

In negotiating with Company A, Steven discovered the high-end salary was the best benefit they could offer. They had a proscribed "track" for career growth, and it would be several years before Steven could move into top management.

Company B was a different story. They couldn't offer as much money as Steven wanted (although they did come up from their original offer), but they were able to offer him a much more flexible, and potentially faster, path to top management.

Before our discussion, Steven was ready to either accept Company A's offer, or to go into Company B and battle for more money. But that wasn't what he needed to make him happy. If he had not clearly determined his goals beforehand, Steven might have made the wrong decision based on something that was not his highest priority.

HOW DO I SET NEGOTIATING GOALS FOR MYSELF?

First, you have to set your limits. You may decide that a challenging job is more important than a high salary, but that doesn't mean you can work for nothing. You have bills to pay, obligations to meet. You have to know what and how much you can comfortably accept. You also have to know where you draw the line; you must determine your absolute cutoff point.

You also need to know the maximum you can ask for—within reason. You can't negotiate by saying you'll accept a lower salary if they'll make you president of the company. That is not a reasonable expectation. You can, however, ask for a better title than the one they were offering you. You start with a reasonable maximum request and negotiate down from there.

SECRET STRATEGY NUMBER 32:
If you ask for too much,
you can always settle for less,
but if you ask for too little,
you won't be able to negotiate for more.

HOW DO I DETERMINE MY PRIORITIES AND MY LIMITS?

Here are some questions you can ask yourself:

- *What do I want to get out of this job?* What are the aspects of the job that attracted you to it in the first place? If you are in a financial hole and are looking for a way to get out of it, then money may be your highest priority. Perhaps you're looking for specific perks other than money. You may want a job in the travel industry, for example, to allow you to visit exotic places. In that case, your negotiations would center more on your ability to obtain time off and reduced travel rates than on a high salary.
- *How does this job fit into my long-term career goals?* You don't want to be shortsighted and accept a posi-

tion because it seems glamorous, or just because the money is good. Does this job lead you toward your goals or away from them? If this job is not in a direct pathway to your goals, are there ways it can help you get there (i.e., by negotiating for a different job title or a specific training program)?

- *What are my real needs (other than money)?* This question refers to both material and psychological needs. You may need time to devote to your family, you may need insurance coverage, or a company car. Your needs may be more in the line of creative freedom or the ability to make your own hiring decisions. Once you've determined your needs, you'll know where you can or cannot compromise your position during negotiations.

- *What is the most I could get?* There is a fine line between thinking big and asking for the most, and being unreasonable and unrealistic. Think about everything you've learned about this company, this job, and this employer. If you've done your homework, you'll know what industry norms are. It may be normal for someone in your position to get a company car, but it wouldn't be realistic to demand a Rolls-Royce. Make a list of everything you want, weed out the outrageous, and use the resulting items as your starting point for negotiations.

- *What is my bottom line?* What is the least you can comfortably accept? Perhaps you can give up the company auto if you get paid for the mileage you put on your personal car. You must know your lowest position, although you never make this information available to the employer. If you tell her your bottom line, she'll go right for it. This is information for you to know so that you won't make an agreement that is not in your best interest.

- *Where specifically can I compromise?* Look at every item on your "demands" list and judge it in terms of necessity and degree. Is this an item you can do without? Is it something you can accept in a lesser version? Suppose health-insurance coverage is one of your necessities. Can you forgo the coverage if you get a salary increase (allowing you to afford to pay for insurance on your own)? Or can you accept coverage for which you and your employer share payment? Once again, you need to know what your ideal would be, and what is the least you would accept.

- *Do I have a clear understanding of what's at stake, what issues are involved?* When you are negotiating, you must always remember, and utilize, your listening and questioning skills. Be sure that you and your prospective employer are communicating clearly. If you're not exactly sure of what's being offered you, say so. You might reply with, "Let me be sure I understand you correctly. You can't offer me a company car, but you will pay for gas and mileage on my car when I use it for company business. Is that correct?"

ONCE I'VE DECIDED ON MY NEGOTIATING GOALS, HOW FLEXIBLE SHOULD I BE?

Flexibility is the key to successful negotiations. When you're in a negotiating session, you won't have hours to ponder each point. You may have to consider new options or change your own ideas on the spot. An employer may offer you an unexpected perk—and ask you to give something up in return. If it's a big issue, you may want to ask to think about it overnight. If it's a smaller item, you should be able to come to a quick decision. It will help you to ask yourself these questions throughout the negotiating process:

- Why is the employer insisting on this particular point?
- Does it affect my bottom line? How?
- Am I still within my acceptable range?
- If the employer makes this particular concession, can I (or should I) give something in return?

WHAT ARE SOME OF THE THINGS I MIGHT WANT TO NEGOTIATE FOR (BESIDES MONEY)?

As we move through the nineties and into the new century, the things we deem important job-related items are rapidly changing. Here are some of the areas for which you may want to negotiate:

Salary	Office space and location
Salary potential	Support staff
Bonuses	Career potential
Commissions	Health insurance
Profit Sharing	Life insurance
Retirement & investment plans	Disability coverage
Pension plan	Child care
Royalties	Parental leave
Performance review dates	Training
Raise schedules	Vacation time
Title	Personal days
Authority	Tuition reimbursement
Responsibility	Company car

*   *   *

THE MONEY QUESTION

Although money may not be your only concern, it is definitely one of your main negotiating points. Let's go back to the opening scenario of this chapter. The prospective employer has offered you $32,000. There are two things you have to know before you can even begin negotiating that figure:

1. *What is your personal bottom line money figure?* How much do you need to pay the rent, pay your bills, and fulfill any other financial obligations you may have? If that figure comes to $30,000, let's say, then an offer of $32,000 might be acceptable (but why not try for more?). If your tally comes to $34,000, however, you're going to have to negotiate.

   You might return to the employer at that point and say, "I know that I would really enjoy this job, and I know that I could make a valuable contribution to the company. But I'm afraid that your offer of $32,000 is not acceptable. Is there room for negotiation?"

   If there is no room for negotiation, you may not be able to accept the job. Negotiating for a different job title or a larger office will not help you pay the rent. If there is room for negotiation, be sure that you initially ask for a figure higher than your $34,000 bottom line so that you can bargain down if necessary.

2. *What is the going rate for similar jobs in this industry?* This is information you also need to know. If others in similar positions in your industry are making $40,000 to start, you know that this employer's offer is not up to par. If the standard is $28,000, then this is a generous offer, and you may not be able to get much more. There are several sources you can use to get this information (check your local library):

- American Salaries and Wage Survey (Gale Research Inc.)
- The American Almanac of Jobs and Salaries (Avon Books)
- The Geographic Reference Report (Economic Research Institute)
- Check your local newspaper's classified-ad section to see what other companies are offering
- Check national publications, such as the National Business Employment Weekly
- Check business magazines that contain annual salary surveys, including:
  - *Working Woman* (January issue)
  - *Business Week* (March issue)
  - *Forbes* (May issue)
  - *Fortune* (June issue)
- Check trade and professional associations for information about salary ranges in your field
- Call the Bureau of Labor Statistics for its annual report "Employment and Earnings" (202 523-1221) or write to: Bureau of Labor Statistics, Department of Labor, 200 Constitution Avenue NW, Washington, DC 20210.

I'VE GOTTEN THROUGH THE NEGOTIATIONS AND I'M READY TO ACCEPT THE OFFER. WHAT SHOULD I DO?

When you accept the offer, review it with your new boss: "I'm pleased to accept your offer. I understand that my title is to be Director of Marketing, my salary is to begin at $34,000 with a review in six months, and I'm to start work on April first. As part of my package I will also receive health and disability insurance, and a two-week vacation after one year. Is that correct?"

SECRET STRATEGY NUMBER 33:
Never settle for less than you want, or less than you deserve.

It's your job. It's your life. Make it a life you enjoy, a life that is fulfilling in all its many aspects. Seek out every opportunity to improve your lot in life. Tune into your desires and go after your goals. Participate. Ask questions.

Questions are the foundation upon which success is built. Successful people who are not satisfied with the status quo don't ask themselves, "Why am I stuck in this situation?" Instead they ask, "What can I do to bring about the changes I want?" Remember, there is no reward for not asking.

SECRET STRATEGY NUMBER 34:
He, or she, who asks for more usually gets it.

CONCLUSION

THIRTY-FIVE SECRET STRATEGIES FOR INTERVIEWING SUCCESS

1. Become a questioning expert.
2. Learn to be *active, not reactive.*
3. Be your own PR firm.
4. Make, and memorize, your personal priority list.
5. Research prospective companies to help you focus on getting the job you really want.
6. Think like a boss!
7. Believe in the value of your own product—YOU—or no one else will believe enough to buy.
8. Your value lies in your skills and experience, and your attitude toward your own self-worth—not in how much money you make.
9. When answering a classified ad, don't apologize for, or even mention, the fact that you lack some of the qualifications listed in the ad.

10. Read the *entire* paper or magazine, not just the want ads, to get interview leads.

11. You're not just going to be interviewed—you're going to interview your interviewer!

12. Never answer an interviewer's question unless you're 100 percent certain you know what it means.

13. Thorough preparation is the cornerstone of self-confidence and the foundation for making a positive impression.

14. Use information interviews to find out both the positive and negative aspects of a job or industry.

15. All networking leads are worth pursuing. Not every lead will turn out to be productive, but you'll never know unless you take the time to find out.

16. The object of a networking interview is to be remembered. You want your networker to keep thinking about you, thereby increasing the possibility that he or she may come up with some other contacts for you.

17. Shop around for an employment agency you like; choose the agency in which you feel the most comfortable. Remember that any agency is only as good as the counselor with whom you work.

18. Since most temporary agencies provide the same services, work only for the one(s) you like and trust.

19. If you want headhunters to call, make your name a household—or industry-wide—word. High visibility is the key.

20. Use your interviews with personnel executives to create an impression, build rapport, and take advantage of their many connections.

21. Sending the right letter to the right person gives you a jump on the competition and makes you a likely interview candidate.

22. If you have to send a résumé, present an image of yourself tailored to the employer's needs and expectations.

23. When making phone contact with a potential interviewer, you're calling as one professional to another—let your manner and attitude reflect your professionalism.

24. Every time you make a call, your goal is to get through to the decision maker.

25. When calling for an interview appointment, set up the expectation that there *will be* a meeting. Give the prospective interviewer a choice between two times.

26. Every question you are asked provides you with another opportunity to sell yourself.

27. Never talk money until you know there is a job offer.

28. There are two objectives to every interview:
    1. Get a job offer.
    2. Get as much information as possible about the job, the boss, and the company.

29. Each time you answer an employer's question, regain control by asking another question.

30. Use your "callback" interview to reemphasize your strong points, and to get in-depth information about the job, the employer, and the company.

31. When you're offered a job, your bargaining power is greater than it will ever be. Use it well and wisely!

32. If you ask for too much, you can always settle for less, but if you ask for too little, you won't be able to negotiate for more.

33. Never settle for less than you want, or less than you deserve.

34. He, or she, who asks for more usually gets it.

35. ASK SMART QUESTIONS. ASK SMART QUESTIONS. ASK MORE SMART QUESTIONS.

INDEX

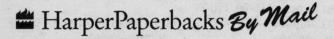

HarperPaperbacks *By Mail*

HarperPaperback's
"RECOVERING FROM SERIES"
For everyone who shares
in the healing process

RECOVERING FROM A STROKE
JUNG AHN, M.D. AND GARY FERGUSON
A straight-forward guide that offers patients, friends, and family members insight into the vital role they play in stroke rehabilitation. A glossary of terms, answers to commonly asked questions, and clear explanations provide a better understanding of what has occurred and prepares the reader for what lies ahead.

Jung Ahn, M.D., is currently Clinical Associate Professor of Rehabilitation Medicine at New York University's School of Medicine.

Gary Ferguson is a science and health writer for national magazines.

ISBN: 0-06-104137-8 $8.99/$11.99 CANADA

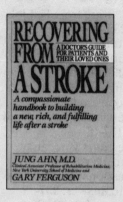

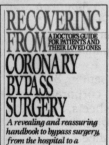

RECOVERING FROM CORONARY BYPASS SURGERY
STEVE G. HUBBARD, M.D.
AND GARY FERGUSON
A revealing and reassuring handbook for the thousands of heart disease patients for whom bypass surgery has given a second chance at life. Dr. Hubbard clearly explains everything patients and their families need to know about the operation, the recovery, and how to vigorously approach a healthy new life.

Steve G. Hubbard, M.D., is a cardiovascular surgeon in private practice in Billings, Montana.

Gary Ferguson is a science and health writer for national magazines.

ISBN: 0-06-104138-6 $8.99/$11.99 CANADA

RECOVERING FROM BREAST CANCER
CAROL FABIAN, M.D. AND ANDREA WARREN

A valuable resource for women diagnosed with breast cancer as well as their friends and family. *Recovering from Breast Cancer* presents an overview of how cancer develops, ways to communicate with health professionals, treatment options, case histories, plus many other important issues. The information provided empowers and encourages the patient living with breast cancer and urges family and friends to take an active role in the patient's recovery.

Carol Fabian, M.D., is Professor of Medicine, Division of Clinical Oncology, at the University of Kansas Medical Center. She is the founder and director of the High Risk Breast Clinic at the university and directs several breast cancer research projects.

Andrea Warren is a freelance writer who specializes in women's health and social issues.

ISBN: 0-06-104135-1 $8.99/$11.99 CANADA

RECOVERING FROM A HYSTERECTOMY
DENA E. HARRIS, M.D. AND HELENE MACLEAN

In this immensely informative guide to hysterectomy recovery, Dr. Harris begins with a tour of the female body and ends with a fearless healing process. Patients and their families come to realize that having a hysterectomy is not the end of femininity, sexuality, or an active life.

Dena E. Harris, M.D., currently runs a private OB/GYN practice in New York City as well as serving as Associate Director of Quality Assurance in the Department of GYN in the infirmary of Beekman Downtown Hospital.

Helene MacLean is a senior writer for *The Child Care Encyclopedia* and a contributor to *Everywoman's Health* and Columbia University's Home Medical Encyclopedia.

ISBN: 0-06-104136-X
$8.99/$11.99 CANADA